Writing Editing

3 Manuscripts in 1 Book, Including: How to Edit Writing, How to Self-Publish and How to Write Content

Jaiden Pemton

More by Jaiden Pemton

Discover all books from the Creative Writing Series by Jaiden Pemton at:

bit.ly/jaiden-pemton

Book 1: *How to Write Fiction*

Book 2: *How to Tell a Story*

Book 3: *How to Write a Screenplay*

Book 4: *How to Write Sales Copy*

Book 5: *How to Edit Writing*

Book 6: *How to Self-Publish*

Book 7: *How to Write Non-Fiction*

Book 8: *How to Write Content*

Themed book bundles available at discounted prices:

bit.ly/jaiden-pemton

Copyright

Under no circumstances will any legal responsibility or blame be held against the publisher for any reparation, damages, or monetary loss due to the information herein, either directly or indirectly.

Respective authors own all copyrights not held by the publisher.

The information herein is offered for informational purposes solely, and is universal as so. The presentation of the information is without contract or any type of guarantee assurance.

The trademarks that are used are without any consent, and the publication of the trademark is without permission or backing by the trademark owner. All trademarks and brands within this book are for clarifying purposes only and are the owned by the owners themselves, not affiliated with this document.

Table of Contents

Book 1: How to Edit Writing

7 Easy Steps to Master Writing Editing, Proofreading, Copy Editing, Spelling, Grammar & Punctuation

Jaiden Pemton

Introduction

When it comes to editing, it is crucial to take your time and be thorough, give attention to the seemingly minor details, and interact with the material on a deeper level to ensure the purpose is being fulfilled. No matter which industry you're working with in the writing world, editing is a universal requirement. Whether you're editing your own writing or serving as an editor for another writer, this guide will show you the top-notch editing strategies, which will be sure to set the content you edit apart in your industry and yield ultimate success as an editor.

It is not possible to predict exactly how many drafts you will need to generate before a piece of writing is ready to go out into the world. Ultimately, the more thorough you are, the fewer drafts you will need to generate. The task of editing requires deep focus and willingness to engage with the content wholly to catch the smallest mistakes, inconsistencies, or areas where the text's purpose is getting lost. Whether you are editing your own writing or someone else's, it is crucial to develop skills that set you apart and help you achieve the most accurate and efficient editing strategy.

When it comes to editing, it is easy to fall into the trap of getting bored or exhausted by the content and skimming over important details. You may reach a point where you have looked over the same words so often. You struggle to determine the right word to use when something doesn't sound right or figuring out how to re-instate the purpose.

You may find yourself feeling so eager to have the content wrapped up and turned in that you start missing small details, which can be a vital mistake. As the editor, it is your job to get the piece of writing that is as close to perfection as possible. If your text is full of errors you did not catch in the editing stage, it will push readers away. This guide will provide you with ideas for maintaining your own energy and enthusiasm throughout the editing process and utilizing tactics such as giving the writing space and editing in reverse to keep a fresh perspective.

In this guide you will find a comprehensive step-by-step reference format with everything you need to know about the editing process. You will be provided with in-depth knowledge of the stages of editing, the importance of reading work aloud, how to manage the small formatting details, how to deeply interact with the content to ensure the message is getting across, and creative strategies you can implement to look at the content differently. Additionally, the guide contains excellent tips for keeping your editing process lively and engaged the whole way through.

The chapters of this guide will take you through each step of the editing journey to help you avoid common mistakes and develop your own thorough process. Each chapter is designed with astounding detail to help you stay on track and address any questions or concerns you have along the way.

Chapters are subtitled and easy-to-follow with examples of tips, tricks, techniques, and things to avoid. Regardless of if you are editing your own writing or someone else's, this guide has all the tools you need to set yourself apart as an expert editor and is sure to serve as the perfect guide to revolutionize your editing experience.

Happy writing!

Chapter 1: Step 1 - Breaking Editing into Stages

As an editor, your role is to make sure everything is clear to the reader. If the reader struggles to read the text, either because it is swaying from the purpose or there are too many mistakes with formatting or grammar, they will have a much harder time reaching the end of the piece. Your job is to advocate for the reader by making their journey through the text as easy as possible and ensuring that they are impacted by the text when they reach the end. To increase levels of clarity and consistency for the reader, you must be persistent in the correction and improvement process. Your role as the editor includes correcting the structure, style, grammar, spelling, punctuation, point of view, and information order. Before you begin, it is vital to familiarize yourself with the client's guidelines (if you are editing for another writer) or the publisher.

Breaking Down the Stages

The editing process includes several stages. The first stage is structural or developmental editing, in which you complete a rough copy edit. Line editing and copy editing are the second stages of the process, and the rough copy edit is the result of this stage. The final step is the fine or final copy edit, which involves final proofreading and preparing for the graphic design and "final proof" stages, which will occur right before publication.

In some cases, if the writer has already done a great deal of initial self-editing on the piece, the structural stage may not be necessary, as the work is already structurally sound. If you are writing and editing your own piece, you will need to make plans to send it on to a professional editor to ensure the work is structurally sound, and then again for the final proofreading. This is because, at some point, you will have been looking at your content so much that you will not be able to target any other edits that need to be made.

Stage 1: Structural Editing

The role of the structural editor is to review the writing from a broader standpoint. The structural stage is not meticulously examining the details but instead considering the text's more significant picture issues. This editor needs to be aware of who the target audience is and the author's primary goal. Editors of fiction stories need to ensure that the plot, dialogue, character, and point of view are clearly expressed and follow the same structure. Editors of nonfiction should examination the general organization of the content and question it for clarity and consistency of the argument and supporting evidence.

Scheduling Structuring Consultations

Suppose the structural editor is not the writer of the manuscript. In that case, they will need to consult with the author to discuss the main idea the author is trying to express so they can evaluate it for clarity. Additionally, the author and structural editor should confirm the style manual that is expected in editing. They should be on the same page regarding the style which will be used, which can be defined in a style sheet. The style sheet is a tool for the structural editor to refer back to throughout the editing process, including all necessary rules regarding punctuation, fonts, headings, capitalization, etc.

Once the editor has come up with a list of structural edits, they will need to meet with the author again to discuss the structural improvements and why they are suggesting them. The structural editor may find that the manuscript is structurally sound and does not need many modifications and, therefore, may advise the author to proceed to the copyediting stage.

Determining the Authority of the Structural Editor

In some cases, the structural editor and the author may agree that the structural editor has full flexibility with their changes, including length, word count, number of chapters, or even the point of view. However, in other cases, the structural editor may be expected to consult with the author to receive approval before making any corrections. Another option is for the structural editor to make all corrections as suggestions in a separate draft and submit it to the client so that all the edits made are visible and can be approved or declined.

Increasing Clarity and Consistency

The structural editor must keep in mind that their job is not to entirely change the manuscript but rather, to make it better. That said, they should move and delete sentences or paragraphs only when it is altogether necessary to increase clarity and consistency. The structural editor can make suggestions on switching the order of chapters, creating new chapter sections, adjusting the table of contents, or creating appendices, descriptions, or introductions.

Focusing on the Bigger Picture

Although the structural editor can correct grammar, spelling, and punctuation, this is not their primary focus. The manuscript will endure further stages of editing, which are more dedicated to these small details. The structural editor should maintain focus on the bigger picture. They should be asking themselves if the way the text is set up is easy to follow, if the theme is being clearly expressed throughout the manuscript etc. If the structural editor is different than the editors who will be working on the manuscript in its later stages, they may choose not to correct the finer details.

Stage 2: Line Editing

The first part of copy editing (the second stage of the editing process) is line editing. The line edit is sometimes called a "rough copy edit" and can only occur after the manuscript has been evaluated for structural soundness. The line editing process does not aim to correct every minor error but rather to continue building on the manuscript's consistency as a whole. The copy editor will check for ways to improve the tone and style to better match the manuscript's goals. If fact-checking needs to occur, the line editing phase is where that will happen. The line reader should fact check information such as places, links, events, and references provided in the manuscript to ensure that the statements are correct. If the manuscript needs an index, it will require a separate "editing pass," which can be done by an indexer or by the line editor.

Addressing Structural Inconsistencies

The role of the line editor is to catch any structural issues which may have been overlooked. If there are remaining structural errors, the manuscript may require further structural editing. The line editor must bear in mind the manual guide chosen for the document to ensure that all of the content is per this manual. The line editor will rely on the style sheet to ensure consistency and add to the style sheet. The style sheet serves as an outline for rules concerning punctuation, spelling, acronyms, capitalization, fonts, and heading and is crucial for creating dependability within the manuscript.

Catching Major Spelling, Punctuation, and Grammatical Errors

As the line editor proceeds through the editing process, they have the authority to make grammatical changes, move sentences and paragraphs around, select deletion of repetitive information, and suggest rewrites for sentences and paragraphs. Their goal is to catch the significant spelling and punctuation errors to improve the grammar of the manuscript.

Conducting Editing Passes

In many cases, the manuscript will pass through a variety of line editing stages. Each stage is considered an 'editing pass,' Each manuscript requires a different number of passes to ensure that all significant corrections have been made. The line editor's role does not extend to correcting minor errors; however, more minor errors may be encountered as the manuscript goes through more passes.

Creating the Final Copy Edit

The final stage of the copyediting process is the most meticulous of all. It is the final stage of corrections before the final design and proofreading stages before publication. If the writing will not be published, the 'final copy edit' is the final stage of the editing process. The stakes are high in this stage, and the process is more detailed.

When copyediting things like newsletters, applications, and reports, which are not going to be published, the copy editor can assume that the document has already undergone self-editing and should not address too many errors. The copy editor strives to catch the last remaining grammatical, punctuation, or spelling errors that were not detected during the initial editing stages.

In the case of a manuscript that will be published, it must receive a final copy edit before it is sent into the final stages of design and proofreading before publication. Manuscripts that need this last copy edit before the designing stage are fiction or nonfiction manuscripts, annual reports, or any other report that will be distributed publicly.

Checking the Manuscript with Fresh Eyes

The copy editor's role is to catch any basic editing that was missed in the line editing stage, using the style sheet and any other manual guides for reference on appropriate stylistic decisions. With fresh eyes, the copy editor will correct any minor mistakes that have not previously been addressed. They will check for any inconsistencies in the text and deal with information such as appendices, index, publication information, and the table of contents that have not been addressed by the line editor.

Preparing for the Final Stage

After the first copy editing pass occurs, the copy editor will work with the author to determine if it is sufficient or needs to go through another pass to ensure no errors. Before the document is turned in or passed on to the design stage, the copy editor must be able to confirm with confidence that there are no errors, and the document is fully ready for the following step.

Chapter 2: Step 2 - Reading Work Aloud

Have you ever been trying to edit an essay with a peer or teacher and been told to "Try reading it aloud?" This is a common editing strategy because it pulls us out of the space of skimming and forces us to engage with the text differently. The process of reading aloud can serve as a useful tool to catch the areas that seem "off" but can be easily ignored when reading the text in your head.

Reading aloud not only builds continuity and confidence with what has been written, but it also helps you to engage with the meaning differently, comprehend what is on the paper, identifying the writing voice, and establishing areas where the flow could be improved.

Significant Benefits of Reading Aloud

There are several significant benefits to reading aloud. The first is that the process of reading aloud helps you to hone in on dialogue and narrative, capture its real authenticity, and ensure that all the right characters are speaking at the right time to keep things flowing. Reading aloud is visual and helps paint a picture in your mind as you read the text, leading you to make changes or say more in some text regions to make these images more potent for the reader.

Reading aloud also yields a more remarkable ability for self-expression. If you are the writer and the editor of your own piece, reading aloud can help establish the connection between your speaking and writing voice. Additionally, reading aloud helps build on your internal listening skills, which can help you tune in to the writing voice of yourself (if you are editing your own work) or the writer you are working for. This can yield more significant success in future writings.

Editing for Clarity and Correctness

In terms of editing for clarity and correctness, reading aloud helps you to sound out words, catch stumbling blocks created by poor punctuation, detect the use of syllables, and catch misspellings. It is much easier to tell if a sentence is a run-on or a word is misspelled if you have the chance to verbalize it. Not only is reading aloud the best way to establish fluidity, build connections, and catch otherwise unnoticeable errors in the text you edit, it can also develop your skills in public speaking.

Reading Aloud as a First Step

When it comes to editing your writing, reading aloud is crucial in catching the mistakes that become easy to miss. As soon as you finish writing your piece, it's a good idea to read it aloud before doing anything else. This is an excellent tactic for catching some initial structural and grammatical errors right from the beginning, which will make the rest of the process much more comfortable. As you read the writing aloud, keep a pen or highlighter handy that you can use to mark areas where you notice yourself stumbling or feeling confused at what was just said.

Establishing Text Flow

When you read aloud, you can establish how your writing flows, how a particular section works (or doesn't work) with the next, and if you are staying in the active voice. One of the best ways to catch passivity is through the reading aloud process. If you find yourself stumbling or getting lost on the message of what you're reading, that is a clear sign that edits are needed.

As you read your work aloud, it becomes clearer whether or not the correct punctuation marks are being used. If you notice pauses, questions, or exclamations in your oral reading, there is reason to believe you should either insert a comma or add a period. If you find yourself going on and on in a single sentence, that's a good sign that sentence is a run-on and needs to be broken up. By listening to your pauses, you can better avoid punctuation errors and run-on sentences. The read-aloud also gives you a process to question your grammar and the meaning of the work. If you don't know what you're reading about, your other readers certainly will not.

Deepening Reader Understanding

To that same token, if you find yourself growing bored as you read, it's a good sign that a particular section needs to be cut.

Boredom while reading is usually a result of the momentum slowing down too much or the writing theme becoming lost to leave the reader asking, "What's going on here and what's the point?" If you feel like a specific section of the writing is slow or confusing, it should either be changed or cut out entirely.

Verbalizing as a Thinking Tool

Saying things out loud about your writing can also be helpful when it comes to remembering ideas for later. If you have an idea but can't write it down, speak it into existence. Listening to yourself talk about it can help form the idea into a memory that you can later take back to your writing desk. Similarly, as you come up with new ideas of things to write or elements to add to your pieces, talk the ideas through with yourself beforehand. It's a good idea to speak these ideas out loud, ask yourself questions the reader may ask, work through inconsistencies and unclear parts, and genuinely engage with the dialogue. In doing this, you can already bring an outside voice to your writing, which can help eliminate ideas that won't get you very far and encourage you to think more.

Personifying Dialogue

Because dialogue is a verbal exchange between multiple characters, the only way to truly measure its efficiency is by verbalizing it. One way to do this is by viewing the dialogue like that of a script. As you read, pay attention to how natural and authentic the dialogue sounds. Does it sound rigid or overly rehearsed? Is each line being spoken necessary? Is there more that needs to be said? Does the correct character talk about each line, or should someone else be saying it? To keep your readers engaged, you must establish this sense of engagement in yourself by reading aloud.

Making Pace Adjustments

Reading your work aloud helps with pacing as it gives you an idea of which parts of the writing are fast-pasted and engaging and where things slow down. Once you have this knowledge, you can question whether or not certain areas are moving too quickly and trying to tackle too much (which can leave the reader feeling confused and strung along) or if they are too slow (which can leave the reader feeling bored and uninspired).

Using your pen or highlighting tool, mark the areas where you notice significant differences in the pacing, and ask yourself if each scene is correctly paced or would be more potent if it was slowed down or sped up. Slowing things down can help the reader take a break from something hectic that just happened or build tension for something wild that is about to happen. Reading aloud is the only way to catch these pacing details.

Honing in on Important Details

Along with improving your pacing, reading aloud also serves to enhance the flow of the writing. As mentioned previously, it is easy for our brains to skip over the seemingly minute details to get to the point of what we are reading. This is especially true if you have been looking at the same piece of writing repeatedly. At some point, your subconscious begins to ignore the finer details. Eventually, even as you read aloud, you may find yourself trying to skip words or move things around. Make a note of these things and ask yourself if your natural desire to do this warrants some sort of change in the text.

Establishing Specific Areas to Edit

Hearing the work you have written read aloud often brings things to light that are hard to notice as our eyes repeatedly scan the page. In the early editing stages specifically, there is a lot more work to be done than we may realize. The writing may be too wordy, too fast, too slow, or lack emotion and passion, have inefficient dialogue, or simply lack interest level. If you are a writer who plans to send your manuscript to an editor to work with, be sure to read it aloud and sort through things first. This way, you can provide more input to your editor on what you need help with. If you are the editor of someone else's work, encourage them to read it aloud beforehand so they can provide more of a basis for discussion. Once it is in your hands, continue to read it aloud until everything sounds right.

Reading Aloud to Others

The final step of reading work aloud in the editing process is to read aloud to another person (or people). The person you read in front of can be anyone from a close friend, family member, or partner, to a peer or even a stranger. Regardless of who you choose to read aloud to, you can rely on the innate appreciation of social behavior to increase your desire to solve problems and pay more in-depth attention to the writing.

Reading aloud is typically a more vulnerable and intimidating experience, especially if you read something you wrote yourself. When we read material aloud, our natural social instincts become heightened because we know other people listen to us and draw opinions from what we say. We have an innate desire to perform well in front of others and receive positive feedback. Your responses will be heightened from this space of vulnerability and slight nervousness, and you may notice things you began to ignore in previous readings subconsciously. You will be extra sensitive to inconsistencies in pace, rhythm, and flow, as well as if a particular section drones on for too long. This heightened sensitivity will allow you to make even more changes and come closer to perfection than you could be reading only to yourself. In this state, you will also have a deeper appreciation for the writing structure, and your desire to produce a pleasing effect will increase.

The heightened sensitivity and social pressure of reading aloud to another person will make the errors in grammar, flow, and punctuation leap out even further, as you will feel nervous about making mistakes. You will be likely to look upon the writing with more meticulous eyes as you consider the fact that other listeners are drawing their conclusions and making their judgments. This will motivate you to solve the problems you encounter within the text as quickly and efficiently as possible.

Chapter 3: Step 3 - Setting Things Apart

When it comes to elements like headings, captions, indexes, appendixes, tables, and contents lists, it can be hard to stay focused. Writers tend to focus more on the main point of what they are trying to say, the characters they develop, and what they want the reader to take away. It is typical for the seemingly fewer essential elements of the writing to slip through the cracks. With the competition of the writing industry and the bustling state of the world, editors cannot afford to be careless with these elements.

Giving Readers Something to Skim

As people navigate their busy lives, they are more likely to skim through writing than profoundly engaging from start to finish. To capture the reader's attention, you must be concise and convincing, drawing them to slow down and engage more deeply with what is being said. When a customer is looking for a piece of content to contend with, they are not reading page after page of the writing itself. Instead, they are looking at the headings, captions, indexes, appendixes, tables, and contents lists to tell them more about what to expect and help them decide if it is worth their time. If a reader is confused by the headings and cannot figure out what will be said in each section, they will have no desire to read that section.

However, if they see even one or two headers that specifically pique their interest, they will be more likely to read on. Readers will be turned off by sloppy captions as well, whereas well-written captions will help them engage further with the content from the start.

Additionally, readers can become overwhelmed by overly detailed indexes or disengaged with overly brief indexes. Although these elements seem small, they serve as the signposts that allow the writer to communicate the purpose of the text, summarize, and highlight the key takeaways. That said, each of these elements is crucial for slowing a reader down in their tracks and drawing them into what the writer has to say. The engagement with these elements should compose at least half of the editing journey.

Tying up Loose Ends

As the editor (of your work or someone else's), it is your job to tie up loose ends and ensure the presented content is clear and well-supported. The hope of every editor of someone else's writing is that the writer will have done some of this work on their own first (for example, by reading aloud).

However, this is not always the case; as many times, the writer will have burnt out from the writing process and will feel that they cannot look at the text any longer. As the editor, you must be able to work with the content in hand, no matter what state it is in. In the cases of editors working for clients, this may look like doing the "dirty work" the writer did not have the energy to do—writing the copy for headings, captions, or any other missing elements. If you are both the writer and the editor, you must be able to enter into a new space in the editing process, in which you are prepared to take on this "dirty work" with a fresh mind.

Conducting Regular Check-ins

After you have checked for grammatical errors, punctuation errors, and spelling errors in the main text, it is good to check for the same things in things like the major headings and the names of people in the manuscript. This check-over should occur in both the manuscript and proofing stages, as errors can be missed even with several editing passes. The last thing you want to happen is to catch these errors once a piece of writing is already published, and the only way to avoid this is by being as meticulous as possible in the editing stages.

Writing Headings and Subheadings

Headings and subheadings must be consistent with pre-established formatting, and they should all look the same (same font, same size, same position, same general length). In general, these elements of all main headings such as chapter titles, 'Contents,' 'Preface,' 'Index,' and 'Appendix' should follow the same model. These headings should be organized logically, separating the text into easy-to-follow sections. Titles should usually have more space above than below them, with spacing varying slightly depending on the heading's importance (for example, a critical heading may be provided with more space, have a larger font sized, and be centered with more space than the average subheading).

Essential articles are marked by the most massive headlines, which should be placed near the top of the page to avoid imbalance. Another tip is to use short words in headings and subheadings as often as possible to avoid confusion that can arise from overusing hyphens.

Not only do headings and subheadings need to be correctly formatted and consistent with one another, but they also need to grab the reader's attention and make them want to read on. In many cases, the writing draft may have some headings in place by the time they reach the editing stage. However, just because the titles exist does not mean they are influential or will serve the purpose of drawing readers closer. Publications will be more successful if they have headers that make a clear statement, impress advertisers, and keep readers feeling hungry for more. If this job is not accomplished in the first drafts, it is the editor's job to rewrite the headers to make it so.

Writing and Editing Captions

When it comes to editing captions, you must remember that even if readers are not engaging deeply with the text's body, they will be naturally drawn to images and pieces of text set apart from the rest in caption form. Captions should be kept short and relevant and should be conclusive with what is happening in the illustration and the surrounding body text. Ideally, the reader will be able to understand what is happening on the page by merely examining a clear-cut caption. As the editor, you must be aware of any cross-references in the text which correspond to illustrations and make sure the figure numbers in the captions line up. It is best to use as few page numbers in cross-references as possible to save yourself the cost and the possibility of requiring further edits.

Dividing the Process into Stages

If you're feeling overwhelmed by the intensity of the editing process, don't worry. There are undoubtedly many things to consider, and the stakes are high for catching as many edits as possible to avoid misprints and ensure the publications' success. That said, there is an excellent technique for keeping yourself on track and preventing overwhelm in the editing stage. This technique involves splitting up each of these "smaller elements" of the writing and focusing on them one at a time. Start with the headings. Confer with your guidelines on which font style, size, and spacing to use in the titles and subheadings, and check them through for consistency. After you have gone over the headings several times, move on to captions. Once again, confer with the guidelines for caption writing.

With each caption, ask yourself if it is clear, concise, and in line with what is happening in the image and the rest of the text. After captions, move on to tables and content lists. Make sure the content lists direct readers to where they need to go to find specific information. As for the tables, make sure the information provided highlights the text's main points or provides the reader with necessary background information (like statistics of case studies).

Next, move on to the index and appendix. Check each one to ensure it contains just the right amount of detail, not too much, and not too little. By breaking up each of these steps and dedicating time to each, you are more likely to catch inconsistencies.

Chapter 4: Step 4 - Utilizing Isolation Strategies

As you move through the editing process, it may become gradually more difficult to tell one idea of the text from the next. After a while, words begin to meld together, and the overall context may become muddled. To keep a clear perspective with each text block, you need to be proactive with text isolation strategies. Later in the guide, we will explore further strategies for maintaining clarity, such as taking space from the text and reading in reverse. However, these strategies generally take place after the manuscript has undergone several editing passes. For this chapter, we will focus on methods of text isolation in the early stages of editing.

Keeping the Focus

Throughout the initial editing process, it can be helpful to use a blank sheet of paper to cover the text you have not yet reviewed. By doing this, you can keep your attention focused on the text at hand instead of looking ahead or becoming distracted. As you finish reading specific paragraphs, make a mark to show that you have looked at them, and don't go back until you are in the next full editing pass.

Breaking the Text into Sections

Another strategy of isolation goes hand-in-hand with the concept of taking space. Depending on your project's length, it is a good idea to establish how you will break up the text before beginning your editing process. It is very difficult to be thorough in the copyediting stages if you don't create small "cut off points" or benchmarks to keep you on track. If you are editing a poem of six stanzas with four lines in each stanza, it would be smart to give yourself about half an hour to work with the material.

Take about four minutes per stanza, with one minute dedicated to each line. You can use this minute to read the line aloud, isolated from all the rest of the poem, to check for flow and word choice. After you have finished all four lines of a particular stanza, take one minute to evaluate the stanza as a whole. Take a moment to breathe, then move on to the following stanza.

Considering Interest Level and Familiarity

On the other hand, if you are editing a 300-page book, the process of text isolation will look much different. You should begin by asking yourself how easy or challenging this particular content is for you to edit. Is it a topic you're familiar with, or is it entirely new knowledge that may take longer to process and could require additional research? Is it something that piques your interest, or is it out of your general interest area and could become tedious as you go along? Is the book written for young audiences and will be a quick and easy read, or is it designed to be intellectually challenging and maybe more time consuming to get through?

Knowing the answer to all of these questions ahead of time will make it much easier for you to understand how to divide the text into isolated sections. Not only will this allow you to be more thorough, but it will also make the process of editing much more manageable. Once you have determined the project's density and your interest level and familiarity, it's time to develop a system for breaking up the text.

Working Through Sections Quickly

If you are familiar with the content in the 300-page book and find it reasonably interesting, you will likely be able to work faster. In this case, you may choose to divide the 300-pages up into ten sections of ten pages, which you can read through fairly quickly. In between each area, take a brief break to look away from the text you just read, leaving it in the past as you move on to a new isolated piece of text. During this break, you may choose to be on your phone, use the restroom, or take a drink of water. Regardless of what you do, make sure to clear your head of the text you just read (besides the general context that you will need to take with you), and allow yourself to move on fully to the next piece.

Determining How Many Sections to Read Per Day

Once you've developed a general system of section-lengths and subsequent breaks, you can decide how many sections to read per day. If each section of ten pages takes fifteen minutes to read, you may choose to do the work in two days, putting in 1-2 hours of work per day. With each isolated section of the text, be sure to give yourself a few moments to reflect upon what you just read, and make notes of your questions and observations to refer back to on the following editing pass.

Working Through Dense Content

If the 300-page book is dense content that is harder for you to understand or feel interested in, you can expect that it will take more time, and you may also need longer breaks in between. You may decide, for example, to divide the readings up into ten-page sections but give yourself 30-40 minutes to complete them. After sitting down for this amount of time to edit a ten-page section, you may find yourself ready for a more extended break, like having a meal, going to exercise, going to a meeting, or merely doing another activity. You can expect this project to be more slow-going and should propose your deadlines as such.

If the sections are denser and take more time and mental energy, you should expect to get through fewer sections each day. Ultimately, it is best to take the time you need to make thorough edits of each isolated area, analyze that section, and carefully write down any notes you have instead of trying to power through the text.

Chapter 5: Step 5 - Interacting for Deeper Engagement

One of the best ways to stay engaged with the editing process is to interact with the text. Interacting with the text can take on numerous forms, from making physical marks on punctuation, grammar, and spelling, to taking a creative spin on reading the story from various character's perspectives. As the editor, it is your job to be fully engaged with the texts at all times, sometimes even more than the writer was. Passivity is a grave mistake in an editor and should be avoided at all costs.

The editor must be a reader who can avoid surface level word processing and truly gain something from the text, to offer meaningful feedback in return. In general, interacting with the text helps editors to avoid falling into passive reading and maintain high activity as they go along. This may look like using the imagination, wondering about further possibilities, asking questions, making analyses and evaluations, and otherwise thinking deeply. Through these tactics, editors will have higher levels of comprehension of what they read. Therefore, they will be able to offer more meaningful edits and suggestions to the writer (or make more meaningful edits to their own writing if they are the writer).

Benefits of Deep Text Interaction

There are several benefits to more in-depth interaction with the text in the editing stages, all of which help make the piece of writing as clear, concise, engaging, and error-free as possible. This deeper interaction helps the editor to think deeply about what they are reading and pinpoint when they feel confused or find themselves drifting off. If the editor feels confused at a certain point in the text, that's a good sign that the author needs to re-work that section of text for clarification purposes.

If the editor begins to drift off and has trouble paying attention to the words in front of them, that's a good sign that the writer should move that section of the text, add more colorful language, or remove it entirely. Text interaction helps to fill in any gaps in comprehension and urge the editor to reflect on both what they have taken from the text and what they anticipate for the future.

Physical Interaction Method

The first method of text interaction is physical interaction. This comes through editing methods, which keep the editor's brain engaged in a particular action system. An example of this would be to develop a table of individual edits to apply to punctuation, grammatical, and spelling errors. Perhaps the editor chooses to place an "x" symbol over every area of the text where there is an unnecessary comma, a circle around areas lacking punctuation, three lines under letters that are incorrectly capitalized, and short underlines under words that should be removed or changed. They may choose to underline or bracket the sentences or sections that capture their attention the most and circle the sentences or paragraphs to find themselves feeling lost or bored.

In terms of spelling, if the editor knows a word is misspelled, they may put it in a circle or box, and if they have questions about the spelling or meaning of a word, they may put a question mark. They could also use arrows to indicate where individual sentences should be moved.

Using a physical symbols system keeps the editor's brain on task while they work and helps them keep from getting lost when they try to refer back to the text. It also gives the writer something to look at so they can see all of the places in the text where the editor found issues. This physical interaction provides the editor with something to do as they read, which is enjoyable and useful for keeping the process on track.

Physical interaction is a deliberate act and can be especially helpful if the editor is working with a piece that they do not find naturally attractive or challenging them more than usual. The physical actions may make the task less daunting, and the editor will have more confidence in what they can do.

Personal Interaction Method

Another method of interaction is personal interaction. To do this, the editor may take the approach of building personal connections with the text by relating it to their own experience or understanding of the world. They may engage with the text by asking particular questions of themselves, such as: "How do I feel when I read this scene?" "What are my emotions towards this character?" "Whose side am I on/Who am I rooting for?" "What do I want the outcome of this piece of writing to be?" "Am I pleased with what just happened in this scene?" "What is confusing to me about this scene?" "What have I learned from this piece of writing?" "What new perspective have I gained?".

It's a good idea to make a list of questions such as these for the editor to answer as they go along. By building these personal connections, the editor will begin to feel like there is more at stake for themselves and their personal life. Their interest levels will be higher, and they will be more intentional and less likely to become distracted. Additionally, their answers to these questions should indicate whether or not the writer has done their job.

Every editor should approach their editing projects with the goal of reading to learn. They should comprehensively analyze the text, integrate new ideas and perceptions, and offer feedback that stems from a place of genuine interest and understanding of what the writer wants to convey.

Chapter 6: Step 6 - Letting Things Sit

Most editors have had the experience of growing bored with the piece of writing in front of them and growing exhausted from reading the same characters, dialogues, and scenes over and over again. This is called burnout, and as an editor, you can almost certainly expect it to happen to you. Editing can be a tedious process, especially once you're a few editing passes in. This is a natural and normal part of the process, but it is not productive. Once you have reached this point, the best way to get back on track is to grant yourself time to step away. Go out and live your life for a few hours, a day, or a few days, without having to think about the editing project at hand. Give yourself a chance to read, engage with other things you enjoy, relax, watch the people and things going on around you, and gain some fresh perspective.

When you come back to the editing process, you can do so with "fresh eyes" and a new perspective for the content in front of you. With this fresh perspective, you will not only enjoy the process more and feel more energized; you will also be able to catch things you did not notice before and offer new critiques. In some cases, you may even find yourself suggesting the writer bring in an entirely new idea or change the focus of individual sections entirely.

Choosing to Take a Break When Frustrated

Looking over the same piece of writing over and over can cause the work to become stale. No editor is unfamiliar with the feeling that comes when you're sitting at your desk, looking at the same project, and nothing is coming forth. Although you know you should have more to say and that there are undoubtedly more edits to make, nothing is coming to you. It is expected that you will start to feel tired throughout the editing process and have trouble focusing as you read the same section for the third or fourth time. You may find yourself beginning to feel frustrated and not know how much more you can do. You may also be dealing with a flustered writer (or, perhaps, you are this flustered writer) who just can't seem to find what "works."

Frustration is usually a good sign that it is time to take a step back. If you find yourself losing sight of the purpose of the writing and the enjoyment in the process of editing it, you will benefit the most from giving yourself a break. If you feel like you have to force yourself through every page, give yourself space from the text to think about what isn't working, get back in touch with your creativity, restore your energy, and bring back some fresh ideas.

Choosing to take a break can save you hours of staring at a screen or page and not comprehending any of the words in front of you. When you take a step back, take some time to remind yourself of the writer's (or your own) purpose in writing this piece. Ask yourself, "What's the point?" and give yourself time to meditate on that while you take a break from it. It's also important not to make yourself miserable throughout the writing process. If you start to feel yourself continuously wrapped up in negative emotions from the stress of editing, do yourself a favor and give yourself some time to rest, breathe, and do things that bring you joy.

Tuning into Your Surroundings

One method for giving your editing space while still gathering perspectives, which will be beneficial when you return, is to tune in to your surroundings when you go out. While you are taking your break from editing, pay particular attention to the people you see around you at the grocery store, in the park, at the mall, or on the streets.

Watch the way they interact with each other; note the way they use body language and the way they engage in daily dialogue. Suppose you're editing a piece of writing that involves character dialogue. In that case, you can take inspiration from the real world to see if the dialogue you're editing sounds realistic and flows well or if it sounds unnatural and hard to follow. As you listen to everyday people engage in conversation, you may realize that some of the dialogue in the piece you're editing sounds too formal or boring. The natural world is full of inspiration, and taking a break to simply inhabit the world can be revolutionary to your editing style.

Strengthening Character Development from Real-World People

This observation of everyday people can also give you more insight to offer the writer on how to develop their characters. You may have the idea of realistic descriptions to add to a particular character to make them seem more relatable, an action they can take that would surprise the reader, etc. You may even have an idea for a new character goal, or a new character entirely, which you can present to the writer (or bring into the piece yourself if you are the writer). Observing a couple in love on a park bench, the exact way they touch each other, how they move their heads to look at each other, and how they speak could form the way you reframe such a circumstance as you edit the writing.

You may see an older woman in the supermarket who reminds you of one of the characters in the piece you are editing. You can take down some brief observations to bring into her character description to become more realistic. As you discreetly observe body language and general human interactions, you may be able to provide further tips for the writer to create scenes the readers can visualize and relate to. The more the reader can visually see what is happening and establish a sense of interest and relatability with the characters, the more inclined they will be to continue reading.

You can play into this interest level by relating the characters in the work you're editing to people you see in your everyday life. If you are editing a piece of writing that involves a motorcyclist named Haven, for example, and you see a woman in a café who rides a motorcycle and reminds you of how the character of Haven may be in real life, you can draw inspiration from the way she drinks her coffee, the tattoos on her arms, etc. In this way, simple observation of real human beings can revolutionize character development and improvement in the editing stage.

Reading for Other Purposes

Another essential thing to do while taking your break from editing is to engage with other author's writing. In many cases, you cannot engage with work you are editing as you would if it were merely a book you picked up off the shelf. The content may be something that is not interesting to you, or you may simply not be able to feel interested because you have too much work to do with finding errors and making suggestions. For this reason, it is crucial always to have something you are reading for pure enjoyment and learning, rather than editing.

As you read the work of other authors you enjoy, ask yourself questions like, "What about this piece of writing captures my attention, and how does the author maintain it?" "Do I care about the characters in this story? If so, why do I care? If not, why not?" "How does the author keep this story moving forward and keep me from becoming bored?" You can improve your editing skills drastically by understanding the techniques used by the authors you like and making similar suggestions to the authors you work with (or applying them to your writing). If you or the author feel like the piece of writing needs something more but can't progress beyond where it is, you can use other writers' work to remind yourself how to bring in extra elements that maintain reader interest.

Move the Mind, Move the Body

Most writers and editors will tell you that moving the body is crucial, especially when your brain is constantly active. Sometimes, your thoughts will become so chaotic and activated that they don't know where to go, and it can become hard to continue the editing process in this state. Mental and physical activity go hand in hand, and you indeed cannot have one without the other. Exercise keeps our brains clear, our moods positive, and our emotions even, which are all critical throughout the editing process's challenges. In many cases, sitting down to edit after a workout is excellent because your mind will be crystal clear, your endorphins will be freely flowing, and you will likely feel more in control and ready to tackle your task.

Editing is a stressful process, and exercise is the perfect way to release that buildup of stress. This doesn't need to get a gym membership or join the community sand volleyball league; it merely means you need to find the way that works best for you to move your body and use it (especially during the editing process). In many cases, a nice jog, yoga practice, dance workout video, or walk around the neighborhood can be the perfect release of endorphins and a way to refocus your brain for when you come back to editing. Whatever type of exercise it takes for you to release your stress, clear your head, and revive your energy, give yourself time to step away and do it.

Giving Yourself Adequate Time

In every step of the editing process, it is important to give yourself plenty of time. If you rush your deadlines and set crunched timelines for yourself, you will not be able to be as clear-headed and thorough. Ultimately, this will result in a less refined piece of writing. While it is easy to become so caught up in the editing process that you feel desperate just to get it done, this can pose a great threat to the work's quality. Be sure not to short yourself on time. Editing is a process that cannot be rushed, and you need to allow for plenty of space to take breaks to make the most intentional edits possible. If you're wondering how long your breaks should be or how much time you should request to meet your editing deadlines, remember that the writing will ultimately benefit from any space you take away from it.

Try your best to keep guilty feelings at bay and value your own time, energy, and general enjoyment in the process. If you are editing for another writer, it is important to have a transparent conversation with them about the importance of breaks and taking space from the writing. Clarify your needs and why you are setting a particular deadline. This will help the author understand your process, which will ultimately put less pressure on you and allow you to do your absolute best.

Redirecting Energy on the "Off Days"

If you sit down to write one day and you feel overwhelmed by negative emotions, lack of motivation, or general disinterest, it's probably not a day you should be writing. In a society that is very driven towards production and meeting deadlines, it's hard to believe it would be okay to change your plans on a day you planned to edit. However, if you don't feel like this is the right day for you to do hours of editing, it probably isn't.

With good planning, you can provide this flexibility for yourself. It's okay for today not to be the right day to edit the way you planned. Instead, decide how you're going to spend the day giving yourself a break, re-cultivating your interest, and drawing interest from the world around you. Just because you're not doing the editing in your traditional process doesn't mean you can't gain experience from reading, taking notes of the things you observe in the world around you, and giving yourself time for the things you need and the things that bring you relaxation and joy. Editing is a draining process, and the more drained you become, the less quality work you will perform. If you sit down and realize today isn't the day for editing, allow yourself to step away, redirecting that energy to a place where it can be productive, then come back tomorrow.

Planning Breaks Ahead of Time

On a typical editing day, it's not a good idea to sit down for hours at a time and try to get everything done. If you do this, your brain may become desensitized to issues with style or other edits that need to be made and start automatically filling in the gaps that need your attention. If you plan to write for four hours, it's a good idea to decide how long your breaks will be within that period. Even if you take just five minutes every hour to stand up, stretch, drink some water, or step outside for a breath of air, your writing process will thank you immensely. You may also try an approach where you write for several hours a day for two days, then take a day to step away. In some cases, however, you may need even longer. Deadlines permitting, you may need to step away for several weeks or even months.

This is especially useful if you are trying to edit your writing and find yourself hitting walls. Give yourself time to live your life, and during that time, you'll be surprised at the new observations, perspective, and energy to bring back to the editing process when you're ready.

Chapter 7: Step 7 - Editing in Reverse

Let's say you have read and edited the same piece of writing several times, and you're beginning to hit a wall. You know that there is more to do, but you can't quite figure it out. You have indicated the writer's main goals, determined where the tension and crisis points are, paid attention to the momentum at various points throughout, made basic grammatical, spelling, and punctuation edits, checked for consistency and clarity, and even read the manuscript aloud. All of the standard editing boxes are checked, yet you still feel that something is missing. This is where editing in reverse comes in.

Overcoming Preconceptions, Deepening Concentration

As discussed previously, your brain automatically fills in the gaps as you edit. When it isn't necessary to focus on every word to get the text's main point, it's common to miss places where the flow is not as smooth as it should be, words are misspelled, or faulty punctuation is used. Putting things in reverse (meaning starting with the last sentence and making your way up) helps to hone your focus on each word and sentence in a new way.

Editing in reverse forces your brain to confront what feels like entirely new information. You will have to slow down and read each word and sentence as if it is the first time you've ever seen it. In many ways, it is the first time you've ever seen it because by reading in a different order, you are automatically unable to operate under the same unconscious assumptions of the plot. The more comfortable you are with the flow of the story and the plot, the more likely you'll be to miss problem areas. Reading in reverse allows you to disrupt this comfort, go against your unconscious assumptions, and genuinely engage with the text with fresh eyes.

When you start from the end, your brain can't assume that "we already know all this," and you will therefore be able to be much more thorough. Each paragraph you read will become an entity that stands alone, which allows you to be more intentional as you examine the sentence structure and words. As you read more slowly and with greater intention and challenge, you will be more deliberate in your editing. Your concentration will deepen, and you will notice the flow of each paragraph in a way you did not before.

Beginning at the End

When you begin the process of editing in reverse, you will want to start at the very end of the manuscript. You may choose to read the pages in the standard order, from top to bottom, but you can read from bottom to top if you want an even more significant editing challenge. By taking each page and paragraph out of context you have become familiar with, you will have to look at each word and phrase and ask yourself what it accomplishes. You will want to make corrections as you go, marking up the paper or making notes in the margins. If you have a new idea for a sentence structure, try it out in the margins. If you're not sure about a correction, feel free to indicate your uncertainty using parentheses or a question mark so you can refer back later on in the editing process.

As you move through the paragraphs, you may choose to choose some method of indicating that you have finished a paragraph, so you don't look at again until the next editing pass. You may highlight a section, mark it with an asterisk, or something else of the sort.

Correcting Consistency, Punctuation, Grammar, and Spelling

Editing in reverse gives you more ability to identify inconsistencies within the text. You may find, for example, that a character is present in a scene they shouldn't be in, or perhaps that a scene is placed in the wrong order. You're more likely to catch these things if you're reading the text in a different way than you're used to. Some of the other things you'll be looking for in the reverse editing stage are punctuation, spelling, and grammar errors.

Identifying Overuse

However, there are several other emphasis areas you should keep in mind, as well. The first of these is the overuse of certain words. Every writer has words they overuse, which can cause the manuscript to lose its flavor. As you read through the manuscript in reverse, highlight, or underline every time the writer uses a similar word. Perhaps they overuse the adjective "beautiful", or the phrase "That being said." After identifying the overused words and phrases, you can easily use a Google search or another simple tool to identify supplementary words and phrases the writer could use instead.

Identifying "Non" Words

Another thing to look out for in the reverse editing process is the use of "non" words. These are the words that can easily be removed without changing anything about the sentence meaning. In many cases, these words are "dead" to the sentence, meaning they make it less impactful and break the flow. There are thousands of "non" words out there, with the words "just," "really," and "very" being just a few.

Drafting in Reverse

In addition to editing in reverse, many editors also find it helpful to draft a reverse outline to check the work. The process of reversal outlining involves taking away all supporting evidence and details and leaving yourself with only the writer's main ideas. You should be able to define these main ideas using bullet-points, which you should ensure are placed in a logical order. This provides a condensed version of the piece of writing, in which the writer can confront if all of their goals have genuinely been met in their main points. After you have generated a reverse outline of the main points you gathered in the editing process, the writer will better understand the places where they need to provide more evidence, expand or condense a scene, or move things around for better organization.

Keeping Author Goals in Mind

The reverse outline cannot be created until the writer has completed a draft and provided it to you to describe their goals. Once you are aware of the goals, you can proceed through the manuscript with a sense of alertness about what is being accomplished in each chapter and paragraph. Before you begin editing, ask the author to present you with a basic outline that lists their writing's main ideas as they understand them. This outline will serve as something to refer back to throughout the editing process and give you something to question. As you begin making your reverse outline, consider using numbers with each bulleted point to keep yourself on track with which paragraph or chapter talks about what.

Answering Crucial Questions

The most critical point of a reverse outline is to answer questions. As you go through each paragraph, section, or chapter, ask yourself if they accurately relate to the author's expressed goals. This strategy will help you catch any scenes or pieces of information that seem irrelevant to the big picture and end up de-railing readers. As you proceed throughout the reverse outlining process, you may find yourself confronting new topics or ideas which are presented throughout the paper and may not relate to the main idea. In this case, the author either needs to change the main idea of the writing itself or remove the irrelevant information.

Another question you should ask yourself throughout the reverse outlining process is where the reader may have trouble feeling on track with the points' order. Are there areas where they may be confused chronologically or feel that they need more information? By asking this question, you can make editing suggestions for how the writer might rearrange the manuscript or individual paragraphs themselves to keep the reader feeling on track and tied into the writing's central theme(s).

As you examine each paragraph, make sure that you do not have any sections repeating the same idea. Although each paragraph should be relevant to the main idea, they should all say something new. If you have two paragraphs saying almost the same thing, it will help combine them, remove one, or revise so that they are each making a different point.

Editing the Specifics of Each Paragraph

It is also essential to make sure that each paragraph stays focused on a single topic. The writer should not try to cover too much ground in a single section; if they do, the reader will more easily get lost. If you identify paragraphs which try to tackle too many things, suggest that the writer separate those ideas to form further paragraphs, or cut the information out if it is not entirely relevant. Lastly, check each section for length requirements. Are they too long or too short? An excellent way to gauge this is by looking at the total number of pages. The longer the piece of writing, the less of a problem it is to have a few longer paragraphs. That said, it is vital to check each paragraph in-depth to make sure that it fits with the flow of the rest of the piece.

Conclusion

When you started this guide, you likely approached it as either the editor of another writer's work or with the desire to edit your writing thoroughly. You picked up this guide with the understanding that in-depth editing is crucial to the overall success of the piece that is being written and that errors in structure, clarity, punctuation, grammar, dialogue, and flow can have a drastically negative impact on how others receive your writing. You were likely aware of all that is at stake in the editing process, especially when it comes to maintaining the interest, understanding, and general respect of readers.

No matter how incredible a story's content is, too many spelling errors, grammatical mistakes, or inconsistencies can ruin the whole experience for a reader. When it comes to the editing stage, you must come prepared for the fact that how thorough you edit the book can make or break the levels of respect, and subsequent sales, it will have. When you edit your work, you should do so not only to create work you can be truly proud of, but also to cultivate a community of followers who have a deep respect for the work you produce.

Throughout the guide, you were provided with the ins and outs of the editing process, from the structural, line editing, and copywriting stages, to the importance of reading aloud, to the seemingly minor details of formatting, to deeply engaging with the content to a point where you can ensure reader impact. You became aware of the risks of missing small pieces if you become careless, and you learned how to be more thorough when it comes to catching these small pieces before it's too late.

You were provided with tips for keeping yourself engaged and present with the work you do. You also learned the benefits of creating a network of friends, followers, trusted writers, and perhaps other editors into your editing process for extra support and perspective. You learned how to maintain a fresh perspective while honoring your own energy by taking breaks, giving the writing space to breathe, taking inspiration from your surroundings, editing in reverse, and creating reverse outlines to clarify the author's main points.

You discovered the importance of being thorough and conducting as many editing passes as necessary to get the writing as close to perfect as possible. You were shown the benefits of reading work aloud to yourself and other people, because hearing it in your own voice can bring attention to details that are easy to skip while reading. You learned how to isolate parts of the text to scan for clarity and cohesivity, as well as how to step outside the original context of the text to slow down and hone in on the smaller details. Additionally, you came to understand some of the best editors' secrets and how to monitor your text for efficiency and full reader engagement.

At the end of the guide, you were provided with fresh ways to work with the text at hand to keep yourself alert and conscious of changes that still need to be made. This will help you save from being burnt out and becoming careless with your editing process. The better job you do as an editor, the more the reader will enjoy their engagement with it, and the more they will search for future pieces by you (or the writer you are editing for) in the future. No matter where you are on your editing journey, this guide is guaranteed to serve as the tool you need to keep yourself on track!

Book 2: How to Self-Publish

7 Easy Steps to Master Self-Publishing, eBook Creation, Ghostwriting, Book Marketing & Publishing

Jaiden Pemton

Introduction

If you are starting with this guide, something has led you to consider self-publishing. You have probably heard of the liberation and total ownership of the self-publishing process, as well as the potential to earn more of your own money. If you are considering whether or how to take the leap into self-publishing, this guide is for you!

When it comes to self-publishing, you must be aware of the industry's ins and outs, the correct terminology to use, how to interact with editors, designers, your fans, network, and target audience, and potential retailers. In modern-day society, publishing is a more ambitious field than ever before, and you need to be on top of your game in order to thrive within it. Whether you're still wondering if self-publishing is for you, or you've already committed to the journey and just need to know where to go next, this guide will show you everything you need to know to thrive within the industry and make a name for yourself as a self-published author. Thank you for choosing to embark on this journey with us.

In order to be an effective self-publisher, you must be prepared to be thorough, intentional, and informed on every step of the journey. Self-publication requires an in-depth understanding of the industry, the genre you are writing in, how to check all the boxes in writing, editing, design, making necessary financial decisions, and marketing and distribution strategies to use.

With the writing industry becoming more challenging by the day, you must be willing to bring high energy to every step of the process. When you embark on the journey of self-publication, you must be clear-headed, driven in your goals, and ready to confront every logistic that comes your way. This guide will provide you with in-depth knowledge of each of these logistics, tactics for managing them, and how to keep your vision fresh in your mind throughout the process.

In this guide you will find a comprehensive step-by-step reference format with everything you need to know about the self-publication process. You will become familiar with the beginning and middle stages of the processes, as well as information to make marketing and distribution decisions at the end of the process. You will learn top secret tips and tricks for writing, editing, title generation, design, description writing, and publication logistics. You will understand how to use social media, build your fanbase, and maintain high audience engagement. Additionally, you will see easy-to-follow lists of key terms, secrets of success, and things to avoid.

The chapters of this guide will take you through each step of the self-publishing journey to help you check all of the necessary boxes and steer clear of any big mistakes. Each chapter is designed with astounding detail to help you stay on track and address any questions or concerns you have along the way. Regardless of where you're at on your self-publishing journey, this guide has all the tools you need to set yourself apart as an expert editor and is sure to serve as the perfect guide to revolutionize your editing experience.

Happy writing!

Chapter 1: Step 1 - The Basic Components of Self-Publishing

There are several significant differences between self-publishing and traditional publishing. Before you make a set decision on which route to choose, it is essential to consider the elements of both. Traditional Publishing requires the use of an agent, a publisher to accept your manuscript, and a contract between the publisher and yourself that allows the publisher to purchase rights to your book. After the publisher has purchased rights, they will assume responsibility for all further editing, formatting, and designing. The money you earn will be dependent on how well the book sells once it has hit the market.

Although you will have to pay less for production expenses and have fewer responsibilities in terms of the fine details, this process is highly competitive and can take a great deal of time. You can expect plenty of rejections from agents and publishers, and even if you land one, you may lose your sense of agency and creative input in how the final project turns out. This means that the book can be designed and edited without your input. In addition, if your book does do well, you will not earn as much as you could earn if you had self-published.

Benefits of Self-Publishing

Although self-publishing requires a lot of work in terms of editing, design, and distribution and may require more money upfront, it is an excellent option if you want to avoid the roadblocks of rejection, loss of agency in your book production, and potential loss of money once it hits the market. In many cases, self-publishing is a great place to start getting your name out there and building a fanbase surrounding your work.

Key Terminology

Once you've chosen to begin the self-publishing journey, there are a number of critical elements you need to be aware of. The most basic of these elements are publishing terms, which you should be prepared to interact with often throughout the publishing process. While you may not encounter all of these terms, it is essential to understand what they mean.

· Barcode → an image that indicates the ISBN and, in some cases, the book's price. Barcodes are machine-readable and are often used by book retailers on print books.

· Copyright → the declaration that the creator has exclusive rights to the publication, distribution, and adaptation of their work during a certain period of time.

· Description → the part of the book that communicates to distribution partners and, later, potential customers what the book is about and how to market it.

· Distributor → the party designated to credit, fulfillment, collections, and in the book industry, selling, on behalf of a publisher.

· E-Retailer → a book retailer who works in an online space.

· Edition → version of a book, many times which has been re-released with corrections or new features.

· ISBN (International Standard Book Number) → Aa13-digit code provided by the ISBN agency of a particular country and assumed by a publisher to demonstrate the format, edition, and publication details of a work. ISBNs are used globally and help to identify book titles and format information quickly.

· .jpg or jpeg. → image files that are most effective for colorful images to be used in the book.

· Keywords → single words or phrases which can be used to summarize the book and make it easier to search for.

· Metadata → necessary information about the book like the price, cover, publication date, author, description, table of contents, etc. which is used by booksellers and buyers.

· On Sale Date → the date when retail partners can start selling a book.

· Page Count → the total number of pages in a book (always divisible by two), including blank pages.

· PDF → Adobe file format which allows for easy creation and sharing of documents that are easy and consistent to print.

· Publication Date → the date a book can be released to retail consumers or libraries to assume possession of.

· Publisher → the person who owns legal rights to the book and makes decisions regarding when it will be available.

· Retailer → any place that sells books (sourced from publishers, distributors, and wholesalers) to consumers.

· Returns → the ability for booksellers to return books to the publisher if they have too many or no longer have use for a particular book. Booksellers must charge publishers the purchase price of the book and will then be reimbursed.

· Status → indicates whether or not a book is available, using terms like "forthcoming," "active," or "publication canceled".

· Subject → used to place books into categories based on content.

· Suggested Retail Price → indication of the price by the publisher.

· Title → information used for reporting and reseller catalog communications.

· Trade → traditional bookselling channels like independent and chain bookstores.

· Wholesaler → a business that is dedicated to fulfilling orders for retailers and libraries with the books they obtain from publishers and distributors.

Although self-publishing can be a taxing process, you can expect to fully control the content and design, marketing, and edits. Your book will likely have increased longevity because no one gets to decide when to stop marketing it. The royalties you save from having to pay a publisher can go into your own pocket instead, and you have the freedom to change the price of your book whenever you want.

Additionally, you have a greater ability to distribute the book worldwide and be in full control of the rights granted to foreign publishers who may want to purchase rights to distribute in their country. Lastly, self-publishing gives you a great deal of flexibility regarding your work timeline and the deals you cut with outside organizations. All in all, self-publishing is a great route for writers looking for independence, agency, and flexibility in their publishing process.

Chapter 2: Step 2 - Beginning Stages

The beginning stages of the self-publishing journey involves bringing your book into existence and getting the essential details underway. The three stages of this process are writing, editing, and generating a title. There are several tools available to help you throughout these processes.

Writing your Book

The first step of the self-publishing process is to write your book. Before you begin, you will need to determine the genre you are writing in. Consider the typical audience of this genre to decide who you are writing to. What kind of writing will pique their interest and keep them engaged? Be sure to pay attention to other relevant works in the genre, such as films, screenplays, and books by other authors, to inform yourself of what does best in the industry.

Writing from this place of understanding and inspiration can help you enjoy the process and ask yourself the critical question: *"What am I trying to say, and how can I say it in a way it hasn't been said before?"* You will need to take the necessary actions of character development, plot development, crafting setting, establishing style and voice, determining theme, making the experience personal, developing a shining moment, etc.

Before you begin to write, you should be able to narrow down what you are trying to say and what impact you want it to have on the readers. If you are writing a nonfiction book, you will need to carve out time to research your topic at great length to ensure credibility. If you are storytelling, you may need to experiment with various organizational techniques, central themes, points of view, and styles to find what works best for you and your goals. Be sure to give yourself space to take breaks, explore, and change things around throughout the writing process, without too much stress or rigidity. Remember, you will have the editing process to work things out any structural or copywriting errors.

Finetuning the Work Through Editing

Although it is possible to edit your book on your own, many self-publishers choose to hire an editor to obtain an outsider's perspective and receive insight on details they may have missed. If you decide to hire an editor, be sure to find one who is comfortable and skilled in your genre. Editors with specialized skillsets can provide invaluable perspective and edits to your writing. Ask yourself what you are looking for in the editor. Do you need an editor who specializes in dialogue? Perhaps you are looking for one to pick apart your structure and organization to ensure good flow. Or, perhaps you need an editor who is skilled in mood development. Either way, make sure you know your editor's strengths, specialties, and comfort level with the material before hiring them.

Making Use of the Editing Process for Your Career

When you begin the editing process, you must bear in mind that this is about much more than the book in front of you. What you learn throughout this process is what you will take with you into the rest of your writing career, and it will help you formulate your future works while learning what to implement and what to avoid. The editing process is your chance to grow by looking back on what you have written reflectively, applying feedback, and developing your writing craft.

If you choose to invest in an editor or editing team, you can consider it an investment in your learning and, ultimately, your future success in writing. Over time, you will see your style, voice, and general writing skill improve. Working with an editor is one of the most remarkable ways to see this transformation happen and may even lead you to create new editions of previous works.

Understanding the Stages of Editing

Before you begin the editing process, you need to know which type of editing you need. There are three stages of the editing process, which are vastly different from each other and all equally important. The first stage of editing is the structural or developmental stage. You determine the big picture of the story and determine if the organization flows well enough to represent that big picture. The following stage is the line editing stage, which is where you begin to narrow the scope, finetuning the language, and making as many smaller edits as possible. This is a stage for a lot of experiments with moving things around, adding new (but relevant) information, or removing parts of the book altogether.

The next part of stage two is copyediting, which involves acute attention to things like spelling, punctuation, grammar, and passive voice. The third stage of editing is the proofreading stage, where you will give the work a few final passes to pick up any errors that may have been overlooked. In many cases, it's a good idea to hire a different editor for each of the three stages so that you can take advantage of their unique skillsets and avoid the risk of them becoming burnt out.

Hiring Multiple Editors

Regardless of whether you or another editor is editing your writing or a combined effort, it is crucial to keep in mind the importance of the editing stages: structural editing, line and copyediting, and proofreading. Begin with big-picture editing passes and work your way down to the most specific details. Because all editors bring different skills and perspectives to the table, your best bet may be to hire a different editor to work with you on each editing process phase.

Making a Good First Impression Through Title

According to experts, the title you choose for your book is one of the key elements that determines publication success. The book's title is crucial to the book metadata and will compose the first impression readers have of the work you have done. The title is the way your book introduces itself to the world. Your title must address a problem the reader has and provide a clear solution(s). Readers should be able to read the title and feel confident about what this book can provide to them and how it can make their life better.

Titles with explicit promises of good results are proven to engage readers. As you create your title, ask yourself what problems your book can solve for the reader, what sort of desirable skill your book will provide, or how your personal testimony and knowledge could make someone else's life better. The title should pique your reader's interest to a point where they can't wait to read more. Seek to capture the imagination of your readers, making them ponder what they might find in this book and how it could change their life. What elements of what you have to say is most fascinating, captivating, or life-changing? What kinds of emotional response do you want your story to produce in the reader? Take your time to brainstorm ideas and test out several titles until you find what works best.

Maintaining Clarity

Your title should be simple, concise, and quickly generated to search engines to increase viewership and revenue. If you are producing a guidebook, you may use the words' how to' in the title to increase the number of hits your book will receive on the various search engines. The words you use should clearly express that you have what the potential reader needs, wants, or desires most in life. Your title should communicate what the book is about and what readers can expect to read about. Statistically, if the book is a guidebook, sales can be expected to go up if the title includes the words 'How to' by providing potential buyers with precisely what they need to know about the book.

Catching Reader Attention

The title of your book should use catchy and creative language that make it unforgettable. Your goal is to establish a sense of character in your book and attract the readers. This attraction method may take on the form of fun, lighthearted language, humor, alliterations, or cleverness. Regardless of which way you develop this title, you should make sure it will roll off the tongue nicely, entice readers, and stick in their minds after reading it. Your title should be appropriate to the genre you are writing in and should be considerate of the target audience.

However, a romance novel's title would use much dreamier and more formal language than a horror novel title. That said, you should aim to stand out from other books in the genre.

Keeping it Concise

When drafting your book's title, be sure not to use any more words than you need to convey the book's theme. The shorter the title, the more likely it will show up in search engines.

Additionally, the title of the book is what will stick with readers for generations upon generations. For titles to be as memorable as possible, they should not be difficult to say or type comfortably. You should strive for a title that is easy to say in interviews and easy for people to pass between one another when recommending your book. The book title should be engaging enough to leave people feeling excited and interested, no matter how many times they have heard it. Do not make the title any longer than it needs to be. You can always expand on your description of the book using subtitles.

Making Use of Subtitles

If you are writing a nonfiction title specifically, it is likely you will not have enough space in the title to express what readers should expect from your book fully. In this case, subtitles can be used to increase clarity. Subtitles should be just as compelling as the title itself and should further expand on the desirable outcome described in the title. You want your title to show readers how your book can address solutions for the pain points in their lives. The subtitle is the perfect place to expand on how this will happen.

Seeking Feedback from Your Target Audience

As you work through the process of title generation, it is important to seek feedback from your target audience. The target audience is the people you are writing to, and they are also most well-versed in other works within your genre. They can tell you what they are looking for when it comes to choosing their next book to read. The best way to do this in today's world is to join a writing group or create your own community via social media. You can utilize tools like a Facebook writing group or a social media poll for the target audience to vote from a series of title options and provide further feedback.

Using Title Generation Tools

If you feel stuck on how to generate your title, there is no need to worry. There are endless options for title generators that can help get you started. Book title generators take what you want your title to express and apply a wide selection of names and formats to choose from. However, it is crucial to be aware of titles that fall flat. In many cases, the titles you generate on a tool should be used more as a source of inspiration than the book's actual title.

Chapter 3: Step 3 - Intermediate Stages

As a self-publisher, your job is to publish your media in the most creative and engaging way possible. The front cover of a book is especially crucial to design. After the title, your cover is the first thing a reader can look at to consider whether or not they will begin to read the book. In this sense, cover design serves a significant purpose in communicating the message of the book. The book cover should include the author's name, the title, and any other elements or images that will intrigue the reader. The book's spine should have the title and author's name for easy identification, and the back cover should list the ISBN, author biography, and any good reader testimonies.

Making Use of the Elements of Book Design

The first element of book design is the front matter, which is all of the information readers will see first. This includes title pages, copyright pages, the table of contents, and forewords, prefaces, and introductions when needed. The second element is the book's body matter, which comprises the book chapters and sections. The third and final element is the back matter, which is the last parts of the book, including epilogues, appendices, and author biographies.

Laying out Interior Book Design

When it comes to laying out the book's interior, you have a lot of layout elements and formats at your disposal.

If you aren't sure which layout format to choose, try examining several of the books on your own bookshelf to find the fonts, layout, and trim size you like best. If you're not sure where to start, consider the following tips:

· Select a legible font and use at least 11 pt. size or larger

· Use 1.5 line spacing for easy legibility that does not use too much or too little space between sentences

· Number the pages of the book for clarity purposes

· Start chapters on the right-hand side of the page

Designing Your Book Cover

As previously mentioned, the front cover is an incredibly crucial element of book design. As you design your book cover or work with a designer who does, make sure to use visually appealing graphics. The cover should use imagery that elicits an emotional response and clearly communicates to the reader what they can expect. Any photos or graphics you use on the front cover should be in high resolution (you can find such images on stock photo sites, many of which are free).

Before diving into cover design, it is a good idea to explore other books' covers in your genre. What style of graphics and font are used for the title and the author's name? What elements are placed on the cover and spine, and what is their general placement? How do the graphic elements of the cover interact with the text? What can the reader glen from the book cover concerning the theme of the book? As you study the books on your own bookshelf, you can better understand the ways book covers should be designed to create a connection with the reader, inflict emotional responses, and lead them to read your book.

Choosing a Professional Designer

Just as it is useful to invest in editors for your self-published book, it is beneficial to invest in designers. People are naturally drawn to images, and the more visually engaging your book is, the more likely readers will be to pick it up. Professional designers are trained to take a topic at hand and represent it in a visually engaging way, and they can often see things that you as the writer cannot. This is why it can be smart to invest in someone who does design for a living. Remember, there are several facets of book design. The first of these is print design, the second is ebook design, and the third is a website and digital media design. Just as it can be beneficial to invest in outside editors for your book, it can help you invest in designers.

In most cases, you cannot expect a single designer to specialize in print, ebook, and Website/digital media design, which may warrant the use of multiple designers. Before hiring a design professional, make sure you have all of the editing finished. After that piece is finished, you can often contact your local Chamber of Commerce or utilize social media to reach out to graphic designers in your area. If you want to hire a professional, there are several things to consider.

First, you should ask any candidates to provide you with a portfolio to examine the style and quality of the work they do and if they have experience with book design. Next, you will need to ask them for a price quote for design work so you can actively plan for that in your budget. After that, you will need to ask them how they handle revision requests and what general process they follow. Finally, you will need to clarify your ownership of the artwork. Feel free to ask for samples of books they have designed for other clients and clarify which program they will be using to do the design work.

Striking a Balance in Description

After the title and the book cover, your book description is likely the next place the reader will go to decide if they are interested in your book. The description leads readers to determine whether this book is worth their time, money, and energy. The description should include just enough information about what happens in the book to captivate the reader and make them hungry to read on. You have to strike a balance between revealing the plot's basis without providing too many details or giving away the ending. The reader should understand the basic setting and context of the story from your description, but they should not know the entire storyline.

When designing the hook sentence of your book description, you need to ask yourself what major issue is at hand in this book. What is the problem you need to solve? Use your creativity to create an engaging sentence that describes the problem that needs to be solved and makes it personal to the reader. Don't shy away from emotion in writing your description—play into it. Play into the main character's fears, suffering, or joys to spark empathy and give the reader a taste of the emotional experience they can expect in this book.

Maintaining Third Person Point of View

Another major thing to keep in mind in writing your book description is writing in the third person point of view. When writing a book description, you should avoid talking too much about yourself. If you do refer to yourself, for example, in a brief author byline, be sure to refer to yourself by your pronouns (he/she/they/ etc.) to maintain the third person point of view. If you include an author byline, be sure it is separated from the rest of the book as a short paragraph after the teaser for the book itself.

Using Testimonials and Endorsements

At the end of your book description, you should use testimonials or endorsements (as long as they enhance the description itself). Testimonials should come from someone who has read the book and had a satisfying experience or found the solution to their reading problem. You can reach out to your fanbase to submit testimonials, and even offer incentives for the best ones.

An endorsement typically comes from an authority figure who your readers are likely to recognize who has read the book and agrees that the content is beneficial, and you are qualified as an author. In many cases, celebrities, popular media sources, or other authors in the genre can be used to provide endorsements.

Practicing Description Writing

The last tip for writing book descriptions is to practice. Draw inspiration from the techniques used by other writers in your genre. Try highlighting different details, using different language, and experimenting with various hooks and conclusions to the description. Make a file on your computer dedicated only to the descriptions of a particular book, and feel free to share it with your network. Remember, it is normal and necessary to have multiple drafts of the same book description.

Revise it as many times as you need to feel like it perfectly describes your book. It is always a good idea to seek feedback from colleagues, mentors, or potential readers to offer their perspective. After they have looked over the description, you can ask them a series of questions to determine whether or not they truly got the message. Based on what they just read, what do they expect the book to be about? What excites them going forward? What areas are still unclear? Do they feel interested in reading on? If not, what could be changed that would pique their interest? Listen carefully to other views, as their suggestions speak to the more considerable reader experience and readers' likelihood to buy your book.

Chapter 4: Step 4 - Costs to Keep in Mind

One of the most critical steps of the self-publishing process is establishing a budget that includes all the costs and that you can stick to. The budget is ultimately up to you; some authors release ebooks as inexpensive as $1,000-$3,000, while other authors may spend much more. Regardless of where you fall on this spectrum, you must understand that all costs associated with publishing the book are your responsibility.

Within this budget, you need to think of people you may need to hire, such as professional editors and designers, as well as technical things like an ISBN, cover photos, copyright, typesetting, your own website, distribution tactics, various advertising and marketing strategies, and other miscellaneous costs. Before you begin your budgeting process, ask yourself how much money you are willing to spend and how well you want your book to sell. While it is possible to self-publish a book on a tight budget, you need to make sure you're not skimping on any details. If you let too many things slip through the cracks for the purpose of saving money, your book will be of lower quality and, therefore, less likely to sell well.

Investing in the Editing Process

Perhaps one of the most essential areas to budget for is the investment in a professional editor. Although it is possible to edit your book on your own, you can create a more polished version of your text if you hire a professional editor (or several) to look over your book and catch any issues with flow, context, spelling, punctuation, grammar, or general content. Even if you are a successful editor yourself, having another pair of eyes to copyedit, proofread, and check your work for consistency can make all the difference in the world.

Because the editing process has multiple stages, you may want to consider budgeting enough to pay editors who specialize in each step. In many cases, the editing stages take up the most considerable portion of costs for self-publishing. Professional editing can cost anywhere between $300-$1,500 on average. If all you need is line editing on a short book, you will probably not have to spend more than $150-$300. However, if you are in need of developmental or structural editing, you should expect to pay much more than that, depending on the length of the book. Additionally, if you choose to hire a ghostwriter, you should plan to spend more.

Investing in Cover Design

Another vital investment to make is in the book's cover design. In some cases, authors are talented in design and choose to design their own covers to make the project even more their own. This can be great for writers who also have particular skillsets in design, but if you are questioning your design skills at all, it's best to either hire someone or invest in a program to help you. If you want to play a part in your own cover design but don't know where to get started, you can access templates and other services on things like Amazon's Cover Creator or licensed images or templates from Canva.

If you are on a tight budget, you can access stock photography options for your cover photo (and any other images throughout the book). If you have a bit more money to dedicate to the cover, you may consider investing in a professional photo shoot to obtain your cover photo. You should also consider whether or not you want a professional headshot on your book cover, as this is an extra cost. Professional cover design typically costs between $100-$600. There are several less expensive options, such as designers who are just starting out and hoping to gain exposure or work that has already been created that you are merely paying to reuse. That said, it is vital to make sure you're not skimping on the cover design. As discussed earlier in the book, the cover is the first impression readers will receive of your book, and it is worth an investment.

Investing in Interior Design

You also need to keep in mind the costs of your books' interior design. This is especially important if you are planning to release a print copy of the book, in which case you should plan to have your text professionally typeset. Typesetting is complex and requires a lot of skill, time, and energy, and you should prepare to make this investment in any print book. If you are releasing an eBook and are searching for customization beyond what you can find on Amazon's Kindle Create, ePub, or similar platforms, you may wish to hire a designer to help.

If you have a larger budget, you may also consider investing in a graphic designer for things like book posters, bookmarks, and business cards. It is a good idea to include general formatting costs in your design costs, ranging from $50-$300. If you're on a tight budget, you may consider looking into free or inexpensive online options for editing book interiors—just be cautious.

If you plan to sell print copies of your book, you should invest in print proofs to double-check the layouts and catch any final errors. IngramSpark can be used for paperback books, and it typically costs $30 per print proof. If you have a team of designers and editors, you will need to invest in a proof copy for each person. If you are printing your book, keep in mind that there will be fees charged by the printers.

Investing in Online Advertisements and Websites

While it is optional, many authors choose to invest in advertisements on social media, magazines, or TV to increase publicity and sales. Some companies assist with marketing and media exposure for a fee. In many cases, authors choose to create a website in which to promote themselves and build a community among their target audience. Your website can serve as an author platform through which to write blogs, expand your business, and gain publicity for your works.

Whether you choose a paid website developer or choose to use a free one like WordPress or Blogger, there are several costs you should be prepared to be responsible for. The first of these is website hosting, which generally costs around $150 per year. You may also need to purchase a domain name, especially if you want to increase the number of people who find your website. The cost for a domain name is relatively low, at around $10-$15 annually.

Lastly, if you want to collect email addresses to compile a mailing list, you will need to pay for an email subscription service. This service will manage all of your emails. In many cases, you can find an email subscription service for as low as $10 per month, depending on how many subscribers you have. If you are hoping to run ads on your website, you should set aside a budget of between $100-$500.

Making Technical Investments

In terms of more technical self-publishing investments, you should be prepared to invest in an ISBN. The ISBN is a unique code that will allow bookstores and libraries to access the book's necessary information quickly. While there are free options that exist (such as CreateSpace and IngramSpark), your book is less likely to be carried in bookstores if you don't invest any money in it. Free ISBNs cause further limitations in that they prohibit eBooks from being stocked on Overdrive, which is a website that circulates eBooks to public libraries worldwide. The cost of getting an ISBN is $295 for 10 ISBN codes, which is worth it when you consider all of the channels of distribution it will open up for you.

Determining Miscellaneous Budget Items

There are several final miscellaneous items to include in your budget. The first of these is the cost to register your manuscript with the Library of Congress and get it copyrighted. You should plan for events such as book signings or release parties and the costs associated with those. Additionally, you should save room in your budget for random logistical items such as shipping, packaging, office supplies, and bookstands. You may also choose to have your book made into an audiobook, which is generally an added cost of between $300-$3,000 (again depending on the length of the book). It is a good idea to have a specific portion of your budget set aside for the miscellaneous items, so you can be prepared to foot unexpected costs if they arise

Budget Planning in Three Categories

As you begin to plan your budget, it's best to divide the process into three categories. First, you should determine what you can comfortably accomplish yourself (while making sure they are still professional and that you can be free of errors). Second, you should evaluate the things you need to pay someone else to do and where you plan to look for those people to hire. Lastly, ask yourself what items you may be able to barter for with friends.

If you have a friend who is a graphic designer, for example, they may be able to help you with your cover or interior design for a discounted price. If you have a friend who works as an editor, you may be able to share your skills with them in exchange for them to do an editing pass on your book. No matter how you choose to divide the three categories in your budgeting process, you need to make sure you have generated an all-encompassing total cost. Once you have determined this total cost, you can determine how many copies of your book you'll need to sell to break even and how many you would need to sell to profit.

Chapter 5: Step 5 - Marketing and Distribution

When it comes to self-publishing, marketing is one of the greatest keys to success. Before you even begin to write your book, you should begin marketing. You should be able to identify the *why,* that is, the reason you are choosing to write this book. You should then identify the *what,* which describes what impact you hope the book will have and what your readers have to gain from it. As previously described, you should be sure to determine who your market is, what they want, and how your book can satisfy that need and create the impact you desire. Once you have answered these key questions, you will have a greater sense of direction in your marketing strategy.

Developing your Marketing Campaign

When you approach the book marketing process, you should do so as you would approach any other businesses. Marketing campaigns take a great deal of skill and attention to detail to accurately portray your audience's gain from your book. How can you help the people who will read your book? How will their life be better after reading it? Once you have answered these questions, you will have a direction for communicating with your readers and making it clear to them why they should read your book.

Investing in Communication

As a self-publisher, you should invest in communication with your readers. This communication can take on many forms. Some self-publishers choose to spend hours researching within their niche and reading others' work, so they know the best and most current tips and tricks to use. Other self-publishers invest time in learning strategies of online traffic keywords to direct more attention to their works. Some spend a great deal of time investing in their social media and generating a following through which to gain readers. Some may opt for a more traditional method of placing their book in physical spaces, such as libraries, bookstores, or other stores and having tables at conventions and other events.

Marketing Using Book Reviews

In many cases, you can use book reviews as a way to market your book. Book reviews use persuasive language and are editorial, not promotional, which makes them appear more genuine. Honest reviews of your book help it be seen for what it is and make it clear to your audience what they are getting into. You can also use author platforms, such as a personal website and your social media accounts. In today's world, online marketing is often more effective and less expensive than traditional strategies.

Implementing a Planning Process

One of the most critical aspects of marketing is the planning process. The most effective planning process has several, which are as follows: segment your markets, target your best customers, understand how, when, and where your customers buy books, and what motivates them to do so, and create a position through which to bring in targeted customers.

Determining Top Markets

When it comes to segmenting your customers, you must remember that it is impossible to check every reader's box. It is essential to understand how different people may choose to use your book and those who are most likely to make frequent investments for their purposes.

You will likely come up with a long list of potential buyers, and you should know that it is impossible to market to all of them equally. From the list, you should come up with your top markets, which will create your targets. Developing your target groups does not mean you are ignoring individuals who are not in those groups; it merely means they are not your focus.

Marketing to the Needs of the Target Audience

As your buyers decide which books to buy, they have a number of things they are looking for. If you are writing a book that targets college-aged voters, you may find that your book would do best in an election year, as tensions are high, and voting is a topic of higher focus. Your target audience may be motivated to buy your book if they know it can tell them what they need to know to form their opinions on voting and have their questions answered.

Your position, then, would be the way you use the topic that motivates your target audience. In this case, you may adopt a position of addressing the fact that college-aged voters may feel intimidated by voting and have questions they are afraid to ask. You can approach them from a place of non-judgment that will help them get all the answers they need to be informed voters in the upcoming election.

Understanding the Buying Process

When it comes to marketing, you should also understand the stages of the buying process. The buying process has five steps: problem recognition, informative search, alternative evaluation, purchase decision, and post-purchase evaluation. Understanding this model is crucial if you want to sell your book.

Problem Recognition

The first step of the process, problem recognition, happens when a buyer realizes they have a problem. In your college-aged voter target audience, the problem is that they feel intimidated about voting and are full of questions they don't know how to get answered. In order to sell your book to them, you must prove why the information within it provides a solution to this problem by answering their questions and equipping them with useful information about voting, so they feel more confident.

You must be aware of the fact that problems vary greatly depending on the market you are working within and the population of your target audience. Nonfiction books, like the one about voting, are geared towards educating the reader and being informative to obtain the desired solution. Fiction books, however, are more focused on solving entertainment-related problems.

Evaluating Alternatives

Once a buyer has discovered they have a problem, they will start looking for a way to solve that problem. This leads to the second stage of the process, which is evaluating alternatives. In this stage, the buyer is thinking of various ways to solve their problem, and they likely will be trying to choose between several books to get the solutions. In this case, it can be helpful to provide free samples of your writing that will give the reader a taste and further implore them to purchase your book.

Making the Right Choice

After they have evaluated alternatives, they will move into a phase of deciding whether or not to make the purchase. At this point, the buyer will be worried about making the right choice. This is an opportunity to follow up with them and encourage them towards the purchase by explaining how it will be worth it and improving their lives. It is imperative not to lose connection with potential buyers during this stage. Overall, you must have a good understanding of your customer's buying processes to plan out your timing.

Adhering to the Buyer's Timeline

Be prepared that customers will all function at slightly different timings, and you should seek to adhere to their schedules. That said, you should be ready to intercept multiple customers at multiple times and in numerous contexts. You may use your website or social media accounts to have giveaways, question and answer sessions, or teasers to keep your readers engaged and promote your work.

Mastering Online Distribution

Equally important to marketing your book in the world, is distributing it. From the time you begin to tell potential buyers about your book, you should be thinking of the most effective ways to get it into their hands. In today's world of technology, you should know that more than half of all book sales (both print and eBooks) take place online. This is crucial knowledge for the self-publisher when it comes to distribution, and it can be used to your advantage in that you have the same, inexpensive access to the online world as any major publishers do. When it comes to book retailers, Amazon is ranked highest globally, no matter the format of the books being sold.

One way to get your book circling online is by creating direct relationships with online retailers. If you are in communication with these online retailers, you will have more control and access to marketing and promotion tools. If you work with eBook distribution services, you will likely have to give up a certain percentage of your profits. However, many of these distributors have access to exclusive promotion and marketing tools, which may help you reach a wider audience and sell more copies.

Determining Print Distribution Options

In terms of distributing print books, print-on-demand options are typically best for new self-publishers. Print-on-demand means that your book will not be printed until after someone has ordered and paid for it. Each order constitutes one printed book, which will then be shipped out to the paying customer. Printing on demand reduces the risk of spending too much money on printing and having many books leftover. That said, it also reduces the likelihood that your book will be sitting on the shelves of popular retailers. It is essential to look at your budget and weigh out the pros and cons when deciding how to distribute your print book.

Making Use of Aggregators

Whether you are planning to distribute digitally or in print, you will want to know how to use an aggregator. Aggregators are companies that allow you to upload your books to a single place, from which they will be distributed to other platforms. Several popular aggregators are Smashwords, IngramSpark, PublishDrive, and Draft2Digital.Out of these, IngramSpark is the one that allows for single uploads for both eBook and print. Most other aggregators require separate uploads to be made. You can use a variety of distributors in combination with other another or separately.

There is no set answer for how many aggregators to make use of at one time. If you have the time and energy, it's a good idea to spread yourself across various individual platforms. When you do this, your royalties will go up, and you may have increased access to things like promotions.

Choosing a Distributor

When it comes to what to look for in a distributor, there are several factors to consider. The first thing you should do is compare the reputations of various distributors. What are other authors saying about this distributor? If the reviews you find are mostly negative or have trouble locating reviews in general, it's best to steer clear. To that same token, you must take into account the reliability of the distributor. Is their service known for reliable content delivery to readers? After you have determined this, you should assess the ease of use of a particular distributor. You want the service(s) you choose to be as quick and painless as possible in terms of digital file publishing and distribution. Lastly, you should examine your budget and compare the cost-effectiveness of various distributors. Make sure to look at every detail of cost involved so you can identify the actual price and compare which distributors are the best value for the money.

Chapter 6: Step 6 - Self-Publishing Mistakes to Avoid

Like in every industry, there are numerous mistakes in the self-publishing field that you should be aware of and take action to avoid. The self-publishing industry is becoming more extensive and more competitive by the day, and therefore, it is more important than ever to be diligent in preventing mistakes.

Being Lazy with Editing

One of the first significant mistakes you can make in self-publishing is to be lazy with the editing process. Grammar and spelling errors, inconsistencies, and clichés may seem insignificant at times, but in reality, these things pose massive stumbling blocks to the reader. Books that are poorly edited are challenging to get through and do not gain the same respect in the industry as their well-edited counterparts.

While there are self-publishers who edit their own work, you have to be meticulous and conduct far more editing passes (with sufficient breaks in between) than you may think necessary. Better still is to edit the book a time or two yourself, then hire a professional editor or editing team for each of the types of editing. Before sending your book out into the world, you must make sure that it has undergone enough editing passes to have every stage of the process completed.

Formatting Incorrectly

Along the same lines as editing, another fatal flaw of a self-publisher is incorrectly formatting the book. It is crucial to make yourself aware of the various stipulations booksellers have in place and abide by those standards in your formatting process. Be sure to thoroughly read the guidelines and note the required file types, graphic formatting, and general manuscript formatting requirements (such as line spacing, paragraphs, and section breaks).

Failing to Reach Out

Not only do some authors fail to have proper editing and formatting, but they also fail to open up the book to trusted members of the target audience to provide feedback. If no one reads your book before it is published, you will send it out into the world with no idea of what your readers will enjoy or the places it still needs work. Friends, family members, and trusted audience members can provide honest feedback and shed light on areas you may not have previously noticed. Better yet is to join a writing community that provides both support and necessary criticism. Not being willing to accept criticism is one major flaw of many self-publishers, and it can truly impact the overall success of that book.

Slacking on Cover Design

Another major self-publishing mistake is making the minimal effort on your cover design. As mentioned previously, the cover of your book is the first impression—it sets a precedent for the rest of the book and helps readers decide whether they are initially interested or not. In an attempt to save money, many authors choose to create their own front covers with minimal design experience. The authors who do this probably assume that the rest of their book will be enough to capture the reader's attention, and therefore, that it's okay to have an average cover.

The problem with this is that if the cover is unappealing, the reader will not even bother to look over other book elements. If you can't hook them with the cover, you have almost no hope of getting them to the next step of the decision process; they will simply rule out your book without a second thought. Therefore, unless you are skilled in design and publishing techniques, the decision to skimp on the cover of your book could completely tank your sales.

Writing a Poor Book Description

Earlier in the chapter, we discussed the importance of a good book description. After the cover, your book description is the next impression of the book as a whole, and you have to make it count. A crucial mistake many self-publishers make is to be boring, rambling, or self-righteous in their description. If readers feel disengaged, lost, or condescended, it is an immediate turn-off from reading the rest of the book. To avoid making this mistake, you should make an effort to read as many example descriptions from your genre as possible. What are the typical structures authors use? What plot points are highlighted? The more familiar you are with these strategies, the more likely you are to engage your reader and set a helpful precedent for the rest of the book.

Losing Sight of the Market

Another common mistake self-publishers make is not taking the time to analyze the market. The best self-publishers know what types of books are selling and why, and they know how to play into those statistics. Not taking the time to conduct thorough research on the market, potential competition, and your demographic can be a crucial mistake. To that same token, not marketing at all is another fatal flaw of many self-publishers. If people haven't heard of their book, they will have no reason to buy it.

As a self-publisher, you must be able to talk about yourself and the work that you do, even before it is published. In a world of ever-growing technology, you will not be able to reach your full potential unless you fully take advantage of marketing via social media. Use things like polls, questions and answers, and teasers to keep your readers and fans engaged with the writing process from start to finish, ultimately giving them no choice but to buy the book when it is released. Identify your personal network of friends, family, followers, and your writing community, rely on them to help you with promotion and buy their book for themselves or gift to other people in their lives. Do not be afraid to ask your support system to promote you.

Releasing Books at the Wrong Time

When it comes to releasing books into the world, timing is crucial. Lousy timing can destroy your book's potential for success completely. Pay attention to the calendar. What season are you releasing your book in? How do members of your audience often react to that season? What is the political and cultural climate? What are the significant events of the day? What are people talking about? All of these are crucial considerations when it comes to the timing of releasing your book. How can the release of your book correspond with what is happening in the world?

Losing Track of Your Release Date

Another major mistake self-publishers make is failing to select and stick to a particular release date in terms of timing. Throughout the marketing process, you must be able to cultivate audience expectations and set the tone of yourself as a reliable person. When arranging your release date, be realistic. Don't push yourself to deadlines you may not be able to reach—give yourself more time than you need to leave room for things to go wrong. If you give yourself this leeway, you can avoid letting your audience down.

Selling your Book for the Wrong Price

When you go to sell your book, another major mistake to look out for is trying to sell it for the wrong price. If the price is too high, people will not only not buy your book but also respect it less. If it is too low, your sales may increase, but you will not be profiting in the way you deserve. Additionally, if a book is priced too low, readers may draw conclusions about the book's quality and assume that it's too cheap to be worth the read. The best way to avoid mispricing your book is to research other books' average prices within your genre. Additionally, it's a good idea to analyze how other authors use promotional discounts and be smart with your personal use to increase your sales.

Limiting Distribution Channels

In an earlier chapter, we discussed the variety of channels through which to distribute your book. While it can be possible to achieve success using only one distributor, this can also be a mistake. In many cases, self-publishers restrict themselves and the book's potential success by using only one channel. To avoid this, allow yourself to use as many distributors as physically possible. What do you have to lose?

Losing Faith in the Face of Failure

The final major mistake self-publishers make to quit if the first book doesn't do well. This is a cutthroat industry, and persistence is absolutely crucial if you want to "make it" as an author. To keep your spirits up, you should view each book you write as an experience from which to grow, no matter the outcome. Each failure is fuel for future success, and you must be patient and persistent. The worst mistake you can make is to give up too soon. Don't rush yourself—take all the necessary actions and then allow things to happen in their time. By doing things right the first time, you can increase your chances for success once the book is out in the world.

When you have finished writing your first book, allow yourself to celebrate what you have accomplished. Writing a book is a massive accomplishment in itself, and one you should be proud of yourself for achieving. With every book you write, you have the chance to develop your fan base, change your strategy, and continue to increase your popularity. Although this chapter has been focused on the mistakes to avoid, it is also important to remember that mistakes are part of the growth process. With each book you write and mistake you commit; you have a chance to try something new the next time.

Chapter 7: Step 7 - Tips for Successful Self-Publishers

In the previous chapter, we discussed the significant mistakes for self-publishers to avoid. This chapter will seek to engage in reframing mistakes to avoid into secrets to apply to your writing process. Throughout this chapter, we will discuss several tips to unlock your most profound potential as a self-publisher, and truly set yourself apart from others.

Taking it Step by Step

The first tip for successful self-publishers goes hand in hand with the mistakes to avoid. As previously mentioned, cutting corners in editing, design, or marketing can abolish a book's potential for success. If your book is sloppily edited, you will lose reader's attention, respect, and level of enjoyment in reading. If you slack on design, your book will be easily overlooked on the shelves, and readers will be discouraged from taking even the first step in engaging with your text. If you are closeminded in your marketing strategies, or worse yet, don't engage in marketing at all, you will have done all of that work only to sell very few copies.

Ultimately, if you choose to go on the journey of self-publishing, go there fully, without cutting corners. By choosing to be thorough in every single part of the process, checking, double-checking, and reaching out for professional help and outsider perspective, your book has the potential to go from good to extraordinary. While it is important to keep costs in mind, you will need to be careful not to sell yourself short. When you set out to self-publish a book, you should set out with the decision to invest in the parts of the process that will enhance your level of success.

Finding Your Niche

The next tip is to be acutely aware of your niche and what kind of content you want to write within that niche. Every human being has particular gifts and passions and a unique life story and way of seeing the world. Perhaps you are a naturally sensitive, hopeless romantic who sees the beauty in nearly every person and place you encounter. Knowing this about yourself, you would likely determine that the place for you is within the niche of romance novel writing. After you have determined that, ask yourself what parts of your perception on romance could make for an interesting story. Locate the gaps that exist in the niche, and ask yourself how you can fill them.

After you have taken time to analyze all of your contributions, passions, interest areas, and experiences, narrow it down to the niche where you have the most to say and will be most well-received. Be sure to keep the context in mind—what element of your story or perspective is most applicable to your target audience? What is the target audience most in need of from your content? Why does the world need this book, and what qualifies you to be the one to write it? Once you have answered these questions, you can effectively narrow down your options to identify your content's best potential niche(s). You can use your target audience's needs to guide your writing process and marketing strategies and cultivate your fanbase and potential for future successes.

Establishing Realistic Goals

Before you begin writing, you should be aware of your personal goals. Why have you decided to set out on this journey? Knowing your purpose and what you hope to provide and gain through the self-publishing experience can more accurately shape your process. Having a clear picture in your head allows you to set realistic goals for your needs and what you hope to achieve. Let's say that one of your goals is to sell a high number of books. You must look at your experience and define "a lot of books" accordingly.

If you are new at self-publishing and have not yet had the chance to establish an audience, you should start a relatively low number and work your way up. Establish a plan for how to expand your author platform, build a fanbase, and market yourself so that your sales can regularly progress. Take time to develop a thorough business plan with daily action steps. What will you do every day to remain consistent with your goals? Take several sticky notes and write your goals on them, then paste them all over your workspace so you can constantly remind yourself the reason for starting this journey, and motivate yourself to stay on it.

Relationship Building and Collaboration

Earlier in the book, we discussed the importance of building your team and trading off skills with friends, professionals, fans, and a writing community. Collaborative relationships open the doors for you to try new things, gain new perspectives and chances for exposure, and cultivate new strategies for success. It is crucial to know who your network is and tap into that. How can your story grow stronger by playing off the insight of your community? Where is your target audience showing up, and how can you meet them there?

In addition to the relationships mentioned, it is also useful to collaborate with outside organizations, non-profits, and community events. You can collaborate with schools, libraries, local bookstores, etc. for book tours, signings, and other events to boost your exposure. You should dedicate plenty of time to researching what's happening with your community, and drafting pitches to various organizations about why the promotion of your book can benefit their organization.

Always Keep Writing

The final tip for self-publishing success is to keep writing, even if you're hitting a wall or feel like the book is finished. Don't let your writing go stagnant—challenge yourself to write a little bit every day, implementing different prompts and techniques. You can keep up with writing by using daily journals, writing entries on your author blog, writing monthly newspaper or magazine columns, or simply sitting down with a pen and paper for a brainstorming session. By continuing to write, you can develop your professional skills and continue to get the word out about the books you've written and the role you play as an author in your niche. Continue to add to your portfolio, book as many events as possible, and remain in a constant state of seeking new opportunities to grow your author platform.

Making a Daily Commitment

When you choose to embark on the self-publishing journey, you must understand that you are making a daily commitment. As a self-published author, you must commit to waking up every day with something new to learn, plan, or complete. You must create a life around who you are as an author and learn to find opportunities for success in every corner of the world. You should view the world as your toolbox, taking inspiration from the people and events around you, as well as the passions, skills, and interests you have been gifted with.

Conclusion

You picked up this guide with the understanding that the self-publishing route was the route you wanted to go and the desire to dive into the logistics of the journey. You likely began this guide with an understanding of the industry's cutthroat nature and the preparedness to learn the details of every part of the process. You understood that in order to be successful, you had to familiarize yourself with the mistakes other self-publishers have made, as well as their secrets to rising to the top of the industry. You had an awareness of all that is at stake in the self-publishing process, especially as it pertains to setting yourself apart from other writers within your genre.

At the start of this guide, you were introduced to the things that set self-publishing apart from publishing with a company. You learned that you have more agency through self-publishing and can call all the shots on marketing, design, and showcasing your creativity. You are in charge of every element of your book, from the beginning of the process to the end, and you can operate freely from publishing companies. When you become a successful self-publisher, there is truly nothing that can stand in your way on your journey to the top.

Throughout the guide, you were provided with the ins and outs of the self-publishing process, from the beginning stages of writing, editing, and generating a title, to the intermediate stages of book design and description writing, to the details of budgeting, marketing, and distribution. You learned the importance of reaching out to other people on a personal and professional level to guide you and make sure you are staying on track with your intentions and appeals to the target audience.

You learned what mistakes to avoid to be as successful as possible, as well as the secret tips of the most successful self-publishers. You learned how to establish yourself as a reliable and well-respected author who regularly engages with their fanbase and keeps the fans involved in the process. You learned how to make your own process and use your creativity, voice, and marketing strategies to your advantage, as well as tips for how and where to distribute.

You discovered the importance of being thorough throughout every step of the process, as well as the benefits of reaching out for help from professional editors and designers. You learned the importance hearing from the target audience members to ask for advice and perspective. You learned that in order to distinguish yourself as a self-published author, you must identify the gaps that exist in your genre and decide how you can fill them. You also discovered the benefits of breaking each stage down into a multi-step process to keep yourself and your team on track.

Throughout the course of this guide, you have learned every skill you need to become a successful self-publisher. With this guide by your side as your trusty self-publishing guide, nothing can steer you wrong!

Book 3: How to Write Content

7 Easy Steps to Master Content Writing, Article Writing,

Web Content Marketing & Blog Writing

Jaiden Pemton

Introduction

When it comes to content writing, it is crucial to be aware of your audience, the needs they have, and how the content you are writing can satisfy their needs and positively impact their lives. This guide will show you how to develop engaging content which will leave your readers feeling satisfied and anxious to come back for more.

In an ever-changing world, there are millions of types of content. Because of this, it can be difficult to set your content apart and prove to readers why they should engage with it as opposed to the other competitors. Within each field of content writing, you can expect hundreds, if not thousands of different perspectives, calls to action and approaches. For this reason, it is crucial to have all the necessary information, know how to talk to your audience, and develop skills that set you apart and help you to achieve the necessary amount of engagement.

This guide will explore the importance of identifying your audience, defining your purpose, and writing content that will excite them and move readers to action. You must understand the logistical necessities of content writing, such as how to present the main ideas, write your conclusion, check your evidence, and edit yourself for technicality purposes. You will also understand how to use your own passion and voice as a way to develop a following surrounding your content, and give readers the feeling of importance within your niche.

This guide will provide you with mistakes to avoid, such as being too broad or narrow, boring your readers, or getting off-topic. You will learn how to avoid cliches and answer all of your reader's questions as they read. You will discern how to check every box in terms of audience questions, concerns, and desires, showing them what they need and how your content can help them get there.

This guide has everything you need to write effective content in a comprehensive step-by-step reference format. You will be exposed to every piece of in-depth knowledge necessary to appeal to your audience, provide the right information, and present a clear call to action. Additionally, you will understand how to distinguish the content you write from other content in your niche, and develop a feeling of reliability and engagement from your readers.

The chapters of this guide will take you through each step of the content writing process to help you avoid common mistakes and develop the process that works best for you and your content. Each chapter is designed with great detail to help you stay on track and address any questions or concerns you have along the way.

Chapters are easy-to-follow with examples of tips, tricks, techniques, and things to avoid. No matter what you are aiming to advertise through your content writing, or who your audience is, this guide has all the tools you need and is sure to serve as the perfect guide to revolutionize your content writing experience.

Happy writing!

Chapter 1: Step 1 - Writing for Your Audience

When it comes to writing content, you must be specific when choosing what information will make it to the page. This decision is heavily dependent on the audience, and the purpose your content aims to fill for a particular audience. Audience interest levels will determine the sorts of statistics, facts, personal narratives, observations, testimonies, and research you should present to your readers. The way you speak about an election process to a room of second graders, for example, is much different than how you would speak about it to a high school civics class or a room of Political Science majors. Understanding the audience is crucial to determining your tone, language, and the general complexity of a particular topic. The tone you select will shape your content and serve the purpose of keeping the audience engaged.

Knowing Your Audience

When it comes to delivering your content, you must have the correct information about your audience to ensure they will be interested and impacted by what you have to say. Consider the election example again. If you are presenting information to a classroom of second graders, you will need to use simple, image-based language and put things into terms that younger children will understand. If you're writing to a high school class, you should assume they have a bit more knowledge due to more experience, but you should not assume that they are experts on the topic.

Advanced figure charts, specified jargon, etc. may not be familiar to these students and may likely end up turning them off. If you're writing for an audience of Political Science majors, you can assume they have higher levels of expertise in the topic and will be in search of more in-depth statistics and terminology. By knowing the level of knowledge, interest, and life experience your audience has ahead of time, you will be able to create much more meaningful connections with them.

Visualizing Audience Reactions

The audience—individuals who will read your content—are one of the major determining factors in how you should develop it. You must have enough information about your audience to visualize their reactions, questions, and what they expect from you. You should have an acute awareness of your reader's interests, hopes, problems, goals, and general characteristics. This knowledge is also important when it comes to digital followers, including unintended readers who may stumble across your content. While invisible readers should not be the major determining factor in the content you write, you should keep some awareness that they may come across your content.

Obtaining Audience Demographics

When it comes to gathering information about your audience, there are several elements to consider. The first element to consider is demographics. Demographics are the data that revealed factors such as age, ethnicity, gender identity, sexual orientation, religious identity, socioeconomic status, and cultural beliefs. Most content writing assignments require an understanding of audience demographics in order to determine what needs to be said and how to say it.

Considering Level of Education

Another element of audience information to consider is the level of education. This applies in the earlier example of writing election content. When audience members have a higher level of education, they will be hungry to read a formal and elevated style with in-depth information and terminology. Conversely, if you are writing to a group of high school students, you will need to be more relaxed and avoid using terms that will cause readers to get lost.

Determining Prior Knowledge

Prior knowledge is also important when deciding how to write your content. You must be aware of what the audience already knows about the topic. Are there any terms or concepts you need to define to make sure your reader understands what's being discussed? How can you feed the knowledge they already have and teach them something new, without going too far over their heads? As a content writer, it's your job to make reasonable assumptions about what your readers already know in order to avoid boring or confusing them.

Defining Reader's Expectations

Lastly, you must be aware of your reader's expectations. What will your audience expect to get out of reading this piece of content? What can they expect to learn? They may approach your content with preconceived notions about the topic and the impact they hope it will have. Additionally, they may have expectations for technicalities like grammar, terminology, formatting, and font. Be mindful of how you title your content, as this will be one of the major determining factors to shape your audience's expectations.

Determining Content Purpose

Once you have determined your audience demographics, education, prior knowledge, and expectations, you can begin to make decisions about the purpose and tone of your content. The purpose of writing a piece of content serves to answer the question *"why?"* If you are writing a piece of content about an election, geared towards an audience of college students, perhaps your purpose is persuading college students to vote. Perhaps your purpose is to create a sense of customer satisfaction in terms of readers feeling pleased with the content they engage with. Or you may seek to fill the void readers feel when they believe businesses do not accurately understand their needs. You may also seek to ease the frustration readers feel by making them feel understood and like the content they are seeing is relevant to their needs. As you develop your purpose, make sure to familiarize yourself with marketing tactics, areas of customer satisfaction and dissatisfaction, and the importance of timing.

Attracting Audience Attention

After you have developed an understanding of who your audience is and the purpose your content will serve, it's time to attract the reader's attention and keep them interested. The world is overflowing with content, and it can be overwhelming to create quality content that stands out. That said, there are a number of tips that can make you a content writing expert in no time at all.

Asking Questions and Sharing Extra Information

Your audience will not be engaged with your content if they don't feel like it is speaking to them. One of the best ways to interact with your audience is by asking questions. Statistically, asking questions of your readers makes them feel important and connected to the content. Asking questions makes readers use their brains to decide whether or not they agree with you, and if they do, this is a good sign that they are being persuaded. It can also be useful to share information about topics related to your content, which will give readers further reasons to engage. Ask yourself how you can produce content that readers will find valuable and lead them towards further action. By sharing further related topics, you can create a sense of community surrounding your audience's values and interests.

Making Use of Written and Video Reviews

Reviews are another excellent way to keep audience members excited and engaged with your content. As a content writer, you should be aware of the best services and resources within your niche, and you can use this knowledge to your advantage. You can gain credibility as a content writer by writing reviews of products, apps, services, and other resources to share information with your audience.

In doing this you can create excitement over tips, advice, recommendation, benefits, and things to stay away from. By that same token, video interviews are another trend that can help you develop yourself as a content writer. You can support the content you write by conducting video interviews where people share their thoughts on the topic at hand. If you can't do interview videos, written interviews can work just as well, and readers will enjoy gaining new information and insights from other readers in the community.

Knowing Your Niche

If you are writing for a particular audience, such as within an academic field or business niche, you should seek to share insights with your readers. What knowledge do you hold about this niche that your readers don't? Take the opportunity to share your insight, along with comprehensive lists of tips and tricks your readers will be excited to listen to. In doing this, you can establish credibility surrounding your brand, business, or topic.

That said, if your audience is broader, you should be careful with being overly specific. If you are writing content (especially website content) and are unsure of your audience's specific expertise, you should aim to maintain a simple, conversational tone. No matter who you are writing to, it's important to keep things concise. No one wants to read long sentences. The longer your sentences are, the more likely your readers are to lose sight of your purpose. It's best to keep your sentences short, clear, and to the point. If your sentences are long, try splitting them up to make them more readable.

Chapter 2: Step 2 - Assigning a Purpose to Each Paragraph

When it comes to reading content, no one likes to read large blocks of text. As previously discussed, it is crucial to maintain a sense of clarity and make your reader quickly aware of your purpose. Content writing should be broken up by paragraph, with a clear purpose and position in each. Paragraphs are designed to split the information up into easy-to-swallow sections—each focused on a single, coherent idea.

All sentences in a paragraph should support the main point. In each paragraph you write, you should establish a clear purpose (*why* this paragraph is being written), the tone (*how* you will convey the subject), and the audience (to *who* this paragraph is addressed). One of the best ways to keep yourself on track with this mission is to start a new paragraph with each new idea you introduce and run each paragraph through a "checkpoint" process.

One of the most common mistakes novice writers make is to write disjointed paragraphs that don't seem to have any relation among them. This can be highly confusing for readers. As such, the aim is to link every paragraph so that you transition from one point to another.

A good rule of thumb is to look at each paragraph as an individual point you'd like to make regarding your main idea. As such, it's a type of puzzle that you are putting together as you transition from one part of the discussion to another. Once you put all of the pieces together, you can articulate an argument that makes sense throughout the passage.

So, let's take a look at the most effective tips you can put into practice as you look to write up your content.

Creating Summary Paragraphs

One major way to condense your content and maintain purpose is by creating summary paragraphs. One of the best ways to do this is to write out all of your information, then condense it into the most important pieces. You get practice summarizing every day in your conversations in class, with coworkers, or friends by describing the major highlights, information, and purpose of what you're talking about.

Summary paragraphs work in a very similar way as you condense larger blocks of text into smaller paragraphs using only the most crucial bits of information. It is important to use your own voice as you craft your summary paragraphs, bringing your personal twist to the most important information in your content. Although it is important to keep things brief, you must make sure not to eliminate any key points or pieces of supporting evidence.

Now, it's important to be careful to not include too much information in a single paragraph. Of course, there is a great deal of value in synthesizing your points effectively. The last thing readers want is for you to go on and on when you could have gotten straight to the point. This is very useful in words of non-fiction. As for works of fiction, you need to be sure that you use the right number of words. By "right amount," we mean that you should take your time to describe points as they are intended to be described. For instance, novels require great depth when it comes to describing scenes and characters. Additionally, novels require you to be thorough when presenting a sequence of events. In the case of non-fiction works, you need to present as much information as you can in as few words as possible.

Do you see the difference?

Please keep in mind that this is a skill that can be developed over time. So, please make sure that you take the time to practice your skills so that you can sharpen them as much as possible.

Quickly Answering Reader's Questions

As you write each paragraph, it is crucial to approach the task with your reader in mind. Remember that your reader will likely be reading your content quickly, and you must respond to their needs within that time. Write the most relevant information, and write for your reader to scan the content. Make sure to conduct thorough research to provide relevant information that will answer your reader's questions and meet their needs.

In non-fiction, it is essential to address readers' questions for the get-go. Sure, you might want to take a few words to introduce the topic and build momentum. However, you will lose readers if you take too long to make your point. Readers want you to get straight to the point. After all, they are looking at your content to find value. This value comes in the form of information. This is something they cannot get if your works are filled with fluff. Naturally, getting to the point is crucial. So, try to avoid beating around the bush as much as you can. Address questions directly. Don't hesitate to economize words and lines. The most important thing is to deliver value every step of the way.

Offering Accurate Descriptions

Although it is important to be concise, you must be sure to offer thorough descriptions of your content. As a content writer, it is your job to determine the services and benefits of the content you are writing on. How can you write about the content in your niche in a way that will stick with readers? What benefits set your content apart? Before you begin to write your paragraphs, take time to make a list of the most important points you will be discussing. Play with several ideas for outlines to determine the correct order of events. How can you adequately transition from one paragraph to the next? How can you use your various research points, narrative tools, and statistics to build up to the largest purpose of the content?

Indeed, furnishing accurate descriptions is about stating the right words at the right time. Now, in novels and works of non-fiction, it might be tempting to describe people and places at length. That's fine only if it leads you somewhere. But if you drag things on for too long, you'll eventually lose readers. The idea here is to provide the right level of detail for the topic you're covering.

Consider this situation.

You are working on a technical handbook. This book requires a good level of detail as you need to accurately describe the elements making up the guide. You need to give readers as many details as possible so that they can carry out the task effectively.

Does this mean you need to write extensively on each element?

Not necessarily. What it means is that you need to ensure that your writing is clear enough so that your readers know exactly what you're talking about. Often, that comes with experience. You may not know exactly how much to write in the early going. However, the experience will show you what a reasonable level of detail would be.

A good rule of thumb is to see things from the perspective of your readers. Think about how you would feel if you were reading it. Your descriptions might make perfect sense to you, but they might not make sense to someone else. If anything, you can always ask someone else to take a look at it for you. That way, you can gauge the effectiveness of your writing.

Narrowing Down Main Points

In the case of the election content, you may decide that your main points are as follows: the statistics of college students who vote, the reasons some students feel discouraged from voting, the issues that get students to the polls, and the ultimate results of young people showing up to cast their votes. By dedicating paragraphs to each of these paragraphs you can accurately keep your reader on track and build up to the primary persuasive purpose, which is to get college students to vote.

In this example, you need to be clear about your points. Otherwise, it might be tempting for you to lose sight of your objectives. When you lose sight of your objectives, you tend to rant and wander away from your main points. This can lead to vague passages that don't address your core arguments. This is why sticking to your argument is crucial when it comes to ensuring effective writing. If you feel that a specific sentence or paragraph does not add anything to your core argument, then drop it. Please remember that there is a great deal of value in always sticking to the point. While it might seem restrictive to some degree, the last thing you want is to be overly vague.

Avoiding Passive Sentences

As you write each paragraph, it is important to survey each sentence for passivity. It is crucial to avoid passive sentences at all costs and keep things in the present tense. Content written in the passive voice is not only less engaging but also more clunky and difficult to understand. By keeping your content in the present tense, you can give readers a greater ability to understand the message and be impacted by it. Passive voice is generally employed in academic and scientific texts. So, it's important to keep that in mind as you go through your overall text.

It's also important to keep in mind that using the passive can get tricky. This is especially true if you build long and complex sentences. This is why the passive is generally limited to academic writing. If you're writing fiction, the passive should be avoided as much as possible. This is especially true if you're writing a fast-paced novel. The passive requires a lot more time to process. Therefore, a thriller needs to stay on target as much as possible.

Please bear in mind that the passive is also very impersonal. This is why it is often used in an academic tone. So, if you're looking to create a warm and inviting atmosphere, using the active voice makes the most sense. In doing so, you can keep things personal and close to your audience.

Chapter 3: Step 3 - Determining Main Ideas and Conclusion

We have discussed the importance of breaking the main ideas into paragraphs, but how do you determine the main ideas? In order to determine the main ideas from a longer passage of information, you must be able to execute a critical understanding of the information. One of the first ways to demonstrate this understanding is by reading the passage thoroughly, then identifying the topic. Who or what is this paragraph focused on? In the example with the content directed towards college-aged voters, the *who* is college-aged voters, and the *what* is the election results.

Summarizing Passages

As you seek to develop your main ideas, you must be able to summarize each passage of information. With every testimony, graphic, or piece of research you read to generate your content, you should aim to summarize it in one sentence. How would you describe the main ideas of each of the informational sources you are using in as few words as possible?

Maintaining Overarching Themes

In the search for the main idea, you should pay special attention to the introductory and concluding information. The first and last sentence of your content should make sense in the overall theme of the content, and the main idea should be expressed. In some cases, you may use the first sentence to set a precedent, then use words such as "but", "thus," or "however" to imply that the second sentence is actually where the main idea lies.

Utilizing Repetition

As you write your content, make sure to provide repetition of common ideas. As your reader reads each paragraph, they should be able to easily summarize what it is about. If they are struggling, they will immediately look for repeated words, phrases, and ideas. Therefore, it is crucial to include this repetition as a guide to keep your readers on track. This repetition leaves the reader with no question of what the paragraph is talking about.

Topic and Thesis Sentences

When the main idea is stated directly, it is called the topic sentence. It is useful to include a topic sentence in each paragraph in order to set the precedent for the rest of the paragraph. The topic sentence should provide a clear idea of what the paragraph will discuss, and it should introduce supporting details readers can look to for evidence. If you have several paragraphs on the same topic within your content, you may be better off using an overarching thesis statement, which you can divide into smaller points throughout the piece.

Implying the Main Idea

If you do not define the main idea in direct terms, you still need to imply it. This implied main idea implores readers to examine the content closely, engage deeply with it, and truly understand what you are trying to communicate. They will pay close attention to the word choice, sentence structure, and image you are painting for them, and this will help them to feel more engaged with the content.

Avoiding Main Idea Mistakes

Now you have learned how to determine your main idea and express it in your content, but there are still several crucial mistakes to avoid. Before you define your main idea, you must be sure to use your skills to summarize the main idea of what you want to express in your content. You can do this through intense research on your topic, and seeking conclusive and persuasive evidence. You must avoid being too broad with your main ideas, while still being sure to provide enough information to your readers.

Revisiting Earlier Information

As you move into the conclusion aspect of content writing, it is important to revisit your thesis or topic sentences that were used throughout. You should model your conclusion after your introduction by referring back to the main ideas and information. Re-explain the evidence, testimonies, statistics, etc. that you used to demonstrate the truth in what you said, as well as what you want the reader to do next. Remind the reader of what they have learned, how it will satisfy their needs, and the role they have in engaging with your content. The reader should have no question of what needs to be done next, and they should feel excited to do so.

Avoiding Introductory Phrases

As you begin your conclusion, it is important to avoid phrases like "in conclusion" or "in summary." Phrases like this are cliché and may cause readers to become bored. As odd as it may seem, it is perfectly appropriate to begin a conclusion without a formal introductory phrase. If you do feel the need to introduce it somehow, you should do so by directing readers back to the evidence they have just read with a phrase like "according to the evidence."

Summarizing the Overall Argument

Your conclusion should summarize your main argument in a short 1-2 sentence blurb that compiles all of the main ideas and crucial evidence you provided in your content. Explain how the statistics, testimonials, or research you provided support the mission you are calling your reader to adopt. What are the things that a particular cleaning product apart from the rest? What are the reasons college-aged students should feel inspired to vote? What insider information can readers get from your posts on the real-estate market that they can't get from competing content?

Facing Opposing Arguments

If you have presented a direct argument as a way to prove the superiority of your content, you cannot shy away from opposing arguments. You have to face the opposition head-on, acknowledge it, and prove why it is irrelevant. In the case of the election example, you may say something like "Although many college students feel defeated by the electoral college and feel that their voices do not really matter, statistics show that their votes are crucial to determining election outcomes." This is the perfect Segway into election statistics you can use as supporting evidence.

Leaving a Lasting Impact

As you draw to the end of your conclusion, you must remember that your goal is to leave a lasting impact on the reader. You should end your piece of content writing with a direct call to action and a statement that will stick in your reader's mind. In order to do this, you should make your readers think, feel excited, and feel that their opinions and efforts matter. You must show why this topic matters, and help the reader to feel the same passion as you do. The reader should have no questions about what is expected of them, or what actions they should take in order to meet their own needs or avoid unpleasantries.

You may benefit from using a "fear tactic" of issuing a warning to further motivate readers. Another tactic is to invoke an image, which will help inspire your readers towards a reality that is better than the one they currently live in. You can add to this by predicting how reality may be shaped if your ideas are implemented. If readers can clearly visualize this, they will feel more passionate to act. Additionally, you may use your final sentence to bring up a universal topic that is easy for readers to relate to.

Speaking to All Crucial Points

As you summarize your content in the conclusion, you should be sure to speak to all of the main points. If you do not take the time to revisit every point you made, you may end up weakening the stance of the content and leaving readers with a muddled image in their head. You should make an effort to provide a general overview of the main points, evidence, and calls to action.

Additionally, you must be sure not to introduce any new information in the conclusion. The conclusion should speak to each aspect of your content, nothing more, nothing less. You need to be creative in the language you use and be sure to provide a thorough recap, but you should not add any evidence or information that has not already been said. If you try to add new information, your reader may lose sight of the main points, thus weakening the overall impact of the content. If you come up with new information that you think absolutely must be added, find a place earlier in the content to add it in, as opposed to simply tacking it on to the conclusion.

Chapter 4: Step 4 - Selecting the Correct Language to Use

When it comes to the language you use in a book, it largely depends on your audience. You cannot expect to reach your audience effectively without using the right type of language. Using the right type of language goes beyond the use of correct grammar. This is about using the language to paint the picture that you want your audience to get. Thus, you need to be sure that the language you use hits home.

Selecting the correct language is about understanding the mind of your readers. As such, your choice of language depends on the factors that you want to convey to them as effectively as possible. If you do this correctly, you will get through to your audience effectively. If you don't, then you might find your audience getting confused or missing the point entirely.

Consider this example:

You are writing an academic paper. Naturally, you expect your audience to be educated individuals with college degrees. As such, it would make sense to use a very formal tone and language to present your paper. Now, imagine you did the complete opposite. You used a vibrant and informal tone. That would lead your audience to stop taking you seriously. Using this type of language would lead readers to believe that you are not a serious and credible source.

Can you see how language plays a key role in getting your message across? Please bear in mind that it's not so much what you say, but how you say it. So, let's explore the elements you need to consider when selecting the language you use in your writing.

Writing for Your Audience

The first thing you need to be cognizant of is the audience you're writing for. Knowing them means to understand who they are, where they come from, and why they would read your writing. Also, you need to know how old they are, their level of education, and what they expect to gain from your writing.

At first glance, many of these elements are pretty straightforward. For instance, if you're writing a children's book, you cannot expect to use complicated language. Depending on the age of the child, you would need to use simple language that isn't tough to understand. By the same token, a book for older kids might have a bit more complex language. Still, you would try to keep it as simple as possible.

There are times when you might have to do a little more research. This is generally the case when you write non-fiction material. Non-fiction material needs to be carefully planned. In particular, you need to know more about who your intended readers are. For example, if you're writing a how-to guide, you need to know if these are novice readers or experienced practitioners. Additionally, you might find that some of your readers are not native English speakers. Therefore, understanding complex language might be tough for them. So, you write with these folks in mind.

Knowing your audience is all about tailoring language and content to suit their needs and expectations. Therefore, it's always a good idea to take the time to reflect on who you're writing for. Doing this will save you a ton of headaches down the road.

Know Your Purpose

It is vital that you identify the purpose of your writing. In short, you must be clear about why you are writing in the first place. Ask yourself these questions:

- Am I writing to inform?
- Am I writing to persuade?
- Am I writing to entertain?
- Am I writing to create awareness?
- Am I writing to debate?

Naturally, the answers to these questions will determine the approach you choose to take with your work. For example, if you're writing to entertain, light and playful tone would serve best. Therefore, you would need to use language that reflects this tone.

Knowing your purpose is an important step in delivering the written message. This is critical in creative fiction writing. If you're telling a dramatic tale, then your tone needs to be serious and somber. If this is a horror tale, then you need to be as "creepy" and mysterious as possible. Of course, that would imply using the right type of vocabulary and sentence structure.

In case you are focused more on an academic tone, then it might be best if you considered using more complex structures such as the passive in order to reflect an impartial, third-party tone. Naturally, this requires you to be more careful with the way you articulate your ideas. Otherwise, you might run the risk of confusing folks.

Selecting the Right Vocabulary

The actual vocabulary you use is dependent on your purpose. This is highly important as knowing your purpose will enable you to make sense of what the language you need to use. Consequently, you will make the right choice when it comes to selecting the proper vocabulary.

Let's consider this situation.

You are writing a thriller. In this type of novel, you need a quick, fast-paced tempo that takes the reader through a long sequence of events in a short timeframe. Therefore, you need to be economical with your writing. So, long and drawn-out descriptions won't fly. You need to keep descriptions short and get to the point of events. To achieve this, you would need shorter sentences in which you utilize lots of synonyms. Plus, you would need to ensure you're using simple tenses and clear sentences.

If you're writing an epic novel, readers will not expect a short book. They will expect you to take them on a journey through a fantasy land. Therefore, you need to be as descriptive and explicit as possible. Here, a voluminous use of adjectives is essential to painting the proper picture you want. As such, there is no need to be economical. You can take as much time as you want to set the scene for your reader. While you might still want to keep grammar simple, it is always best to make sure that you don't skimp on the details. When it comes to novels, the devil is in the details.

As you can see, your approach depends on the type of audience, purpose, and message you want to convey. You cannot expect to make a thriller move swiftly by taking the time to stop and smell the roses. By the same token, you can't expect your audience to fully imbibe your epic tale by rushing them through the events.

Selecting the Right Tone

When we talk about "tone," we're talking about the way you choose to say things. In spoken language, the tone is about the inflections in your voice. The tone is also about the speed in which you speak, and the type of accent you place on your words.

In the case of writing, the tone is all about the level of formality you use. Also, tone pertains to the way you frame the information readers get. When you hear about tone, you often see words as "academic," "lively," "serious," and "humorous." All of these words provide an indication of where your book is headed. As such, ensuring that you have the right tone depends on how you want to present your information.

Let's assume you're writing a fiction novel. Your intended audience is young adults aged 18 to 25. Since you know your audience, you know they prefer a light and informal tone. They don't want you to use highly sophisticated words. They want you to keep it simple and to the point. This means that you choose to use commonly used words, short tenses, and mainly in the active voice. You make sure that you don't use long and complex sentences that cause the reader to overly think about their meaning. As such, you want a crisp and fast-moving read. These types of books work well for people on the go.

Now, let's assume that your targeting older readers. So, you're writing a novel that deals with the struggles of life. As such, this is a very mature topic that requires a great deal of reflection and insight. Naturally, you can't expect to have a quick-paced book. You need to take your time to properly present your point, develop your arguments, and state your positions clearly. In the end, you bring about a conclusion that makes sense to the reader. In this example, you can afford to take longer to express your point, while using more complex language and structure. After all, chances are that your readers aren't necessarily on the go. Thus, they can afford to dedicate a little more time to reading.

Ultimately, the tone is about ensuring that you build the proper atmosphere. As such, you can use it to bring the reader into the right state of mind. As you build your argument, you can then drive the point home directly and effectively.

Staying True to Your Personality

One of the hallmarks of all great writers is the ability to let their true personalities shine through. Often, this means using their real voice when writing. Some writers are witty, while others are insightful. Then, you have passionate writers, while others are straight-shooters. The fact is that you need to let your voice shine through your writing. Trying to be something you're not is a sure-fire way of getting stuck. The most prolific writers can produce a great deal of content because they don't hide who they really are.

The first step to letting your personality shine through is to write the way you think. Now, this is easier said than done. It is often difficult to articulate your thoughts in a manner that's comprehensible to others. Yet, it's important to reflect your thought process in your writing.

Consider this example.

Let's suppose you're writing a romance novel. Now, you are not a naturally "romantic" person. Instead, you're more rational and down to Earth. As such, attempting to be poetic is not something that comes naturally to you. So, if you try to be as poetic as you can, you might find it very difficult to get through your novel. In contrast, if you stick to your true self, you'll find that you can put an interesting twist into this novel.

The aim here is to give yourself a chance to be who you are. Don't pretend to be something you're not. Being authentic is about using your words to describe one particular thing. Sure, others will have a different way of describing the same thing. Nevertheless, being able to let your particular voice shine through is essential to creating the right mindset in the reader.

This is what the best writers are capable of.

They transport you to their thought process. In the end, they are able to help you navigate through the maze of thoughts and ideas that lead to the ultimate outcome. Now, readers may not agree with the outcome. However, readers signed up for the trip and not necessarily the outcome. As such, it's your job to take them through a journey they will enjoy every step of the way. You can achieve this by letting your voice shine through. Don't allow yourself to get caught in being "perfect." Unfortunately, that's what a lot of writing classes intend to teach. There is no such thing as perfection. Language is an art that's intended to reflect your individuality. So, make every effort to let that individuality manifest itself.

Chapter 5: Step 5 - Providing Evidence

One of the biggest challenges that writers face is backing up their claims. This is especially important for non-fiction writers. After all, the last thing you want to do is mislead your readers. Providing misleading information is a sure-fire way of getting yourself discredited. Thus, the challenge becomes finding the right ways to back up everything you write.

Providing evidence becomes a question of producing honest and unbiased information. Ideally, you'd be reporting facts. That way, any ideas you share have the proper backup. This will lead you to become a trusted source in your particular area of expertise. Of course, there is no question that we all have our own opinions and biases. In many cases, readers expect you to make your position evident. That is why backing up your work as much as possible is essential to ensuring that you are not just throwing things out there.

As a pro, you need to become aware of the various tools you can use to back up your claims. Mainly, these devices will provide you with the tools you need to position yourself effectively in your area of expertise. So, let's get right down to it.

Why Back Up Your Claims?

There is a difference between fact and opinion. Facts are essential to building a credible argument. Facts provide a solid means of establishing a reasonable foundation for your entire argument. If you fail to do so, your readers might dismiss you altogether. While your writing might be solid, your argument might be flimsy, at best.

So, backing up claims is essential to building a reputation in your chosen area. When you back up everything you write, you instantly vault yourself into another level. This is especially true if you're challenging common beliefs and ideas. Being able to bring forth new ideas with the right sources is a great way of creating content that resonates with readers.

For non-fiction writers, providing facts enables readers to get the right information they need. As you provide them with credible sources, your readers will come to expect the real deal from you. They will come to know that you're not just pulling ideas out of a hat. Your readers will know that you have taken the time to do the research. In the end, the information you provide is filled with valuable information they can rely upon.

As for opinions, please ensure that your opinions are also based on facts. The last thing you want is to put opinions forward that doesn't have any reasonable backing to them. While they may be perfectly logical and consistent, opinions that lack backing gets dismissed or discredited. Ultimately, your opinions won't carry as much weight as well as researched ones. So, it pays to do your homework.

Not All Sources Are Created Equal

It is very important to note that not all sources carry the same weight. Mainly, sources are only as good as their credibility. Therefore, you need to ensure that whomever you cite has the right amount of weight behind them. If you cite sources that don't necessarily have a good reputation, your claims won't be taken seriously.

In the academic world, your sources are vital to ensure you have the right kind of backing. For example, scientific journals, university publications, and peer-reviewed materials are all valid materials to choose from. By the same token, reports from the mainstream media all provide adequate support for your claims, especially when describing events.

In contrast, if you choose sources that don't have adequate backing, then you are risking the validity of your claims. Even if you're assumptions are correct, the sources you cite will discredit your work. As such, you need to make sure you have the sources in mind. For instance, if you cite conspiracy sites as opposed to reputable news agencies, your materials won't have the same level of credibility. By the same token, solid sources may lead you to fine-tune your arguments as they may provide you with ideas and information you hadn't considered. Whenever possible, do a cursory search on academic databases, scientific journals, or mainstream media sources. The better the reputation of your sources, the more credibility your work receives.

Also, quoting subject matter experts is a great way of giving your materials the credibility they need. When you use expert opinions, please make sure that the context fits the overall scheme of your materials. One of the biggest mistakes is to cite an expert only to realize that their opinion somehow contradicts your arguments. Now, if you're using a contradictory opinion for the sake of framing an argument, that's fine. However, please make sure that if you're using expert opinions to support your claims, these had better be in line with what you are trying to achieve.

Types of Sources

Let's take a look at the various types of sources you can use to support your work. Please bear in mind that you want to ensure they come from reputable places and individuals. That way, your work will have the backing it needs to be taken seriously.

Scientific Journals

If your content is academic in nature, then scientific journals make all the sense in the world. You can search for individual journals to see what articles they have published on your chosen topic. Also, you can sift through academic databases. These databases group articles on specific topics published in various journals. That way, you can get a glimpse into the type of literature that's available out there.

Now, there is one caveat to scientific journals. Journals have varying levels of popularity and acceptance. As such, journals are ranked based on their reputation, standing, track record, and quality. So, it's a good idea to do a Google search to find the best-ranked journals in your chosen area. That way, you can start with publications from those journals first, and work your way down. That way, you can be sure that your sources will be taken seriously.

Whenever possible, try to avoid citing studies and papers through the media. For example, you cite a study discussed in a newspaper article. However, it would be much more effective to seek the study itself and use that as your source. The reason for this is that you can get the information you need straight from the source. The last thing you want is to report information that's already been filtered by someone else. After all, you can't be sure that another writer shares the same opinion as you do. Therefore, it makes sense to go straight to the source.

Case Studies

Case studies are a great way to find examples of the point you are attempting to illustrate. Often, case studies provide real-world situations that demonstrate your point. Also, case studies generally show how a theory can be seen in practice. That way, you can show readers how your arguments can be seen in real life.

Another way you can use case studies is to distill key points from them. When you go through one, you can find important lessons, experiences, or concepts that you can use to get your point across. Then readers will use your case study as a means of mirroring their own assumptions. As such, a case study serves to make your point. It is a means of independently verifying what you are looking to prove.

There is one caveat with case studies. Make sure that the circumstance surrounding it is relevant to your audience. For example, if the case study was conducted in a country that's very different from that of your readers, they may have trouble relating to the situation surrounding it. So, please ensure that case studies are as relevant as possible to your readers.

Testimonials

Testimonials can be a bit tricky to use, especially if they don't come from the most credible sources. In particular, testimonials from regular folks work well with advertising. However, if you're looking to back your materials, you might be better off using expert opinions.

When you use a testimonial, you need to be careful about the specific topic you're discussing. For example, if you're talking about a highly scientific topic, then you might be better off sticking to academics and subject matter experts. Now, if you're reporting facts about a specific event, then definitely witness accounts and testimonials from people directly involved are very good places to start.

In the end, testimonials can serve to prove a point, especially when you don't have first-hand knowledge of the situation. First-hand accounts very useful when you're writing a journalistic piece. As for works of fiction, you might be able to incorporate these testimonial accounts within the overall scope of the story. The main point here is to ensure that you maintain credibility. Some authors like to clarify the fact that they are presenting witness accounts and not expert testimony.

On the subject of expert testimony, such accounts from experts during court proceedings, congressional hearings, or sworn statements are all good sources of information. Since these opinions are given under oath, the individuals who furnish them need to be as forthcoming as possible. Unless these expert witnesses flat-out lie, you can be sure that you have a trusted source of information.

News Reports

You need to be careful when it comes to the media. It's important to note that the media doesn't always get it right. Of course, there are trusted publications that have an impeccable reputation. However, that doesn't mean that their work is absolutely perfect. Whenever you use journalistic works are your sources, it's always a good idea to make sure you double-check whatever is stated in their publications. It could be that news reports leave out something important or perhaps miss and key point. As such, you want to make sure you double-check. Otherwise, someone might call you out on your claims. Needless to say, that is something that you want to avoid.

When you look at journalistic works, always try to verify their sources. If you see things such as "a source spoke on a condition of anonymity" then you're dealing with hearsay. While the outlet might be reputable, the information itself cannot be independently verified. Therefore, that opens the door to unnecessary scrutiny. This is why it's always important to verify the information yourself before confidently using it in your material.

Interviews

If you have access to experts and witnesses, you can use interviews as a means of backing up your work. Ideally, you would have full permission from the individual to use their accounts freely. That way, you can use their name as a means of backing up your claims. Most experts are willing to do interviews free of charge. However, you would need to be patient and as transparent as possible.

If you use second-hand interviews, it's always a good idea to contrast the same information from as many sources as possible. Often, media edits interview to fit their airtime or particular agenda. As such, finding unedited versions whenever possible is always a good way of ensuring the quality of the information you present.

Please ensure that you avoid taking interviews out of context. This is rather easy to do, especially when you have a specific bias that you want to pursue. Unless the overall interview fits your narrative, it's always best to be fair. Taking statements out of context can seriously damage your credibility and reputation. Therefore, try your best to use the types of materials that fit your narrative so that you can maintain a consistent narrative throughout your materials.

Chapter 6: Step 6 - Triple-checking Technicalities

Quality is crucial when producing effective materials. In addition to appropriate tone, vocabulary, descriptions, and arguments, you want to ensure that you have the right grammar, spelling, and cohesion. All of these elements are fundamental to producing high-quality content.

Much of this process is done in the editing phase of your content. Editors can help you spot inconsistencies in your arguments, paragraphs, or ideas. Editing is not meant to bash your work. Instead, it's meant to clean it up so that your ideas truly shine through. Otherwise, you could find yourself making needless mistakes.

It's also worth noting that polishing up writing shows readers that you care about them. After all, if you take the time to make sure your work is spic and span, they will feel that you are serious about your work. Naturally, it doesn't matter how good your writing is. If you're sloppy, readers will call you out on it. So, it makes sense to pay attention to detail as much as possible.

So, let's take a look at how you can triple-check the finer points of your writing. In the end, you want to make sure that you put your best foot forward. This will make you seem like the real pro that you arc.

Checking Grammar

Grammar is one of the trickiest parts of writing. While there is no question that you can speak the English language appropriately, using proper grammar in writing can lead you to feel out of place at the time. After all, it's one thing to have a conversation, while it's another to write down your ideas clearly and appropriately.

So, checking grammar is crucial to ensuring the right type of material you want others to see. For example, verb tenses can be tricky at times, especially when you're building long, complex sentences. Naturally, it's easier to keep it simple. When you do so, you ensure that you're not making things harder on yourself. In the end, keeping sentences short and clear is always the best way to go.

You ought to be the first line of defense with grammar. You must take the time to ensure that you're using the proper form every time. However, human error is quite possible. It could be that you simply make a mistake. Therefore, the second line of defense is useful. You can enlist grammar-correction software to help you navigate this part. Grammar-correct software uses artificial intelligence to ascertain proper writing. This type of software gets it right most of the time. Of course, it's not perfect. Yet, it can work pretty well on its own.

Lastly, getting an editor to go through your work is highly recommended. Now, you don't need to employ a professional editor or proofreader. Often, a friend or family member can help you spot things you might have missed. As such, it is always a good idea to get another pair of eyes to go through your writing. That way, you can be sure that you're getting things triple-checked effectively.

Ensuring proper vocabulary

By "proper vocabulary," we're not talking about cursing. Instead, we're talking about using the right words you need to get your point across. Many times, the right vocabulary may be technical in nature. In such cases, you might need to get someone specialized to have a look at your content.

There are other times when you might need someone to double-check the way you use specific words. For example, you might use one word or phrase too often. Therefore, having someone else go through your text would reveal such inclinations. In the end, the other person going through your text can help you find other ways of phrasing your ideas.

Proper vocabulary also refers to things use as the use of prepositions, conjunctions, and interjections. These words may be easily corrected by spellcheck software. However, it's worth noting that no software is perfect. Therefore, it's important to have a pair of human eyes to go over your text. This is how you can triple check your efforts.

If you're not confident in software, you can always have two different people go over your text. Sometimes, having two completely different individuals review your text can provide you with a good sense of how well written your text is. The idea is to be as thorough as possible. Being thorough is all about ensuring that the words you are using are being used in the proper context.

Beware of Sounding Smart

A common mistake is attempting to sound smart. This action refers to using words, phrases, and structures that make your writing more intricate than it has to be. Now, there is nothing wrong with using a formal or even academic tone if the situation warrants it. However, it is entirely different when you take a regular text and try to make it sound more complex than it should be. Many times, this is the result of feeling insecure about your writing abilities. Naturally, writers attempt to overcompensate for their perceived lack of originality or talent. However, that could not be farther from the truth. The aim is to let your voice sound true as much as possible.

When you think about your content, it's crucial to write for your audience. Thus, it's critical to avoid trying to impress your audience. When you try to impress others, you get away from your strengths. As such, you won't give yourself the proper opportunity to let your voice manifest itself.

To avoid this situation, try your best to have others judge your writing. The idea of judging is not to "pass" or "fail" your work. The aim is to have others see if your work is a true reflection of who you are. From there, you can feel confident in your ability to make your voice manifest.

Use Beta Testers

The term "beta testing" refers to running real-life trials with a finished product. The aim of a beta test is to determine how real customers react to a specific product. In the end, customer feedback is used to make any final tweaks to the product prior to its final launch.

Beta testing is very common in the software world. However, you can use it for your writing, as well. Conducting this type of testing is quite straightforward. All you need to do is to take your writing and have other folks read it.

That's all.

Then, you offer them the opportunity to critique your work. You can offer them the opportunity to provide you with freeform feedback or a more structured approach such as filling out a worksheet. Either way, your beta testers can offer you insight into the effectiveness of your writing. This feedback can give you a sense of how well you've used vocabulary, terminology, and tone. This type of testing goes beyond the mere act of double-checking grammar and spelling. This is about understanding how well your work resonates with your intended audience.

Please remember that a combination of machine and human intelligence is a great way of polishing up your writing. However, please make sure you don't take things personally. Many times, writers take critique personally. Many times, there is nothing personal. It's just a question of people providing you with an honest take on the impact your writing causes. Ultimately, you always have the opportunity to go back to the drawing board to perfect your work.

Chapter 7: Step 7 - Utilizing Your Passion and Your Voice

Passion is one of the elements that cannot be taught. Passion is all about making your voice manifest throughout your writing. This is the ingredient that great writers are able to make manifest in their work.

When you think of the best writers in history, they are all able to let their true voice shine through regardless of the topic in their writing. For example, great novelists can take seemingly pedestrian events and turn them into great works of literature. Other incredible writers can take run-of-the-mill topics and present them in a lively and entertaining manner.

Making your passion evident is far easier when you actually feel passionate about a topic. But what if you're not really into a topic? What if you're merely writing because you need to? Think of all those school papers you've had to write. How passionate were you about those papers?

Using your voice to manifest your passion is crucial in making your writing stand out above the rest. Your passion is what takes readers on a journey through the various elements needed to go from good to outstanding.

So, let's take a look at how you can use your passion to make your work stand out above the rest.

Make Your Position Clear

When you attempt to make your passion manifest, you must state your position clear. Sometimes, that means taking sides in a debate. Other times, that means staying neutral. The point here is that you want to let your readers know where you stand from the get-go. You can't reasonably expect your readers to take part in your passion if you flip-flop from one position or another.

Let's consider a couple of examples.

First, you're writing an academic work. In this work, you can state your side of the debate. You are forthcoming about your opinions, thereby leading the reader to know what side you're supporting. Also, it could be that your position is to remain neutral, that is, you're not supporting any side in the debate. As such, you present facts, state an argument, and then state conclusions based on your findings. This is a common practice among academics.

Second, you're writing a work of fiction. To make your work that much more personal, you openly take a position as part of your book's narrative. So, you let your narrative reveal what position you have taken. For instance, you're writing a romance novel in which there are clear heroes and villains. Also, you're writing a historical novel in which you seek to expose the wrongdoing of certain individuals in a series of events.

In both cases, you are presenting your position directly to the reader. The difference lies in the way you do it. When writing non-fiction, you can afford to get straight to the point. In fiction writing, you have the luxury of taking the time to get to the point. In either case, the idea is to ensure that you have a clear mindset as you write.

Avoid Becoming a Cheerleader or a Critic

When passion becomes manifest, it can be easy to get carried away. Mainly, you might find yourself singing the praises of a person or events, while you might bash other folks or situations. While we're not advocating that you always remain neutral, it's important for you to state your opinion with a clear and level-headed approach.

Let's consider both sides of the equation.

Firstly, when you favor a specific position, it's vital to state your support and then outline the reasons why you support this position. Then, it's essential to back up your supporting points. Otherwise, you may come off as a cheerleader. Of course, people who agree with your position will be happy to follow along. However, those who do not agree with you might become turned off. Therefore, you want to avoid turning people away. Doing so needlessly risks losing readers.

Secondly, when you oppose a specific position, take the time to explain why you don't favor your position without resorting to needlessly bashing your object of criticism. When you open bash other people and positions, you might come off as bitter or resentful. Needless to say, that is not what you want to portray. If you're clearly opposed to one thing or another, it's essential that you state why you oppose the situation with a clear and consistent argument.

Maintaining a level-headed approach is often hard for professional writers. Allowing your personal bias to remain clearly away from your statements is a must. Therefore, you must ensure that whatever you write, you are always on the same track. Most of all, you need to ensure that your statements and claims are fundamentally true. Otherwise, you risk becoming discredited.

Writing for Fun

For some, writing is a job. For others, writing is a passion, a hobby, a pastime, if you will. For people who truly enjoy writing for the love of it, writing comes a bit more naturally. Writing for fun then becomes an enjoyable task. This is something that often comes through in your words. Unless you write on a topic you hate, your general enthusiasm will peer through your overall work. Readers will be privy to your passion for writing.

This is a rare treat for most readers.

Think about reading the news. Journalists are often detached from the information they report. They merely stick to the facts. Moreover, journalists have templates and formats they follow to ensure they are accurate in their reporting.

Now, compare a run-of-the-mill news report to an editorial. In an editorial, you'll find the writer is truly passionate about the opinions they present. While they may try to remain objective and professional about the position they take, these writers clearly manifest their passion. They do so because they enjoy what they write. To them, writing is an exercise in self-expression.

So, look at writing as a means of expressing your personal individuality. Your readers will come to know the real you from the way you use words to express yourself. Perhaps you might not be the most articulate speaker, but you can definitely use the power of written words to make your readers jump into your psyche.

If you approach writing as a job, please be sure to find a system to help you automate your writing process. There are plenty of courses and systems out there. However, we're going to talk about one approach that's highly successful.

First, begin by briefly introducing your topic. A short background description is enough to give readers a glimpse of what they can expect in the text. This will enable readers to prepare their minds for the upcoming discussion.

Then, state your position. Try to be as clear and objective as possible. Try to avoid using colorful language that makes you a cheerleader or a critic. Also, try to avoid any inflammatory or overly enthusiastic remarks early on.

After, let your readers know that you will present your supporting evidence for your position. Whether it's a work of fiction or non-fiction, you can take the rest of your content to fully develop your argument. As you do so, make sure that you clearly outline your position as logically and consistently as possible. Please try avoiding leapfrogging from one point to another. This will only confuse readers.

Lastly, provide a conclusion in which readers can get a summary of what you have just told them. The practical purpose of this conclusion is to give readers something they can take away with them. From there, you have used a system that you can automate every time you write.

Please keep in mind that writing ought to be an enjoyable process most of the time. If you find it tough to write, don't sweat it. Often, it's a question to find the right time and mindset to produce content. The most important thing is to dedicate time to writing. In the end, you'll be able to produce your very own works much faster than you could have ever imagined.

Conclusion

When you started this guide, you likely had a product or service you were interested in advertising through content writing, and you had the desire to set yourself apart in the content writing industry. You were likely aware of all that is at stake in making your content stand out and motivating your readers, especially in a society that is brimming with new content at every turn.

Throughout the guide, you were provided with the ins and outs of the content writing process, from how to determine your audience, to maintaining engagement, making the main points stand out, introducing and concluding effectively, answering reader's questions, developing clear calls to action, and double-checking technicalities. You learned tactics for remaining consistent and reliable and building a name for yourself through your unique passion and voice.

You learned the benefits of building a community surrounding your content and making readers feel involved and important. and your content by creating a community. You learned how to address common questions and concerns to further develop your credibility and reassure your audience as they engage with the content you write. You became aware of the most common mistakes to avoid, such as being too broad, too narrow, introducing irrelevant information, or forgetting to revisit important points.

You learned how to acknowledge what your readers need, what makes them feel satisfied, and what inspires them to act. Additionally, you learned what kinds of language to use when addressing unique groups, and you developed tactics for keeping readers from getting confused or bored halfway through.

This guide has helped you discover how to capture and maintain reader engagement, as well as how to increase levels of excitement and inspiration in your community of readers. Throughout your content writing journey, this guide is sure to serve as your toolbox to guide your every move.

So, the time has come for you to go out there and show what you're capable of. Indeed, becoming a proficient writer is a question of time and practice. Nevertheless, you have everything you need to get started on your path to perfection. With each passing line and paragraph, you will perfect your craft. Eventually, you will be able to reflect your voice clearly and effectively. Your readers will come to appreciate your contributions.

Ultimately, you will discover that writing is an action that involves joy and satisfaction. Finding your inner voice is crucial to transmitting the message you want people around you to hear. As you develop your own voice, your readers will become attached to your specific brand of writing. This is what differentiates the best writers from the rest of the pack!

More by Jaiden Pemton

Discover all books from the Creative Writing Series by Jaiden Pemton at:

bit.ly/jaiden-pemton

Book 1: *How to Write Fiction*

Book 2: *How to Tell a Story*

Book 3: *How to Write a Screenplay*

Book 4: *How to Write Sales Copy*

Book 5: *How to Edit Writing*

Book 6: *How to Self-Publish*

Book 7: *How to Write Non-Fiction*

Book 8: *How to Write Content*

Themed book bundles available at discounted prices:

bit.ly/jaiden-pemton